"The acknowledged heavy hitter in the field of family travel."

The New York Times

"Solid vacation-planning advice and an eclectic mix of family-friendly nature destinations—some that will surprise you."

Christine Loomis, *Family Life*

"As far as family travel is concerned, Dorothy Jordon has been there and done that. *Great Nature Vacations with Your Kids* is an invaluable, extremely readable, totally knowedgeable resource for everyone, whether your idea of experiencing nature involves roughing it or being pampered.

Nancy Clark
Deputy Editor, *Family Circle*

"This book is a gold mine of ideas, information and practical suggestions for enriched family vacations. It details a multitude of programs to ensure that your children learn from nature and enjoy it, too.

Paul Grimes

When it comes to traveling with children, Dorothy Jordon is the Pied Piper of tour guides. The next time I leave home with my daughters, I am going to one of these kid-friendly destinations.

Jack Bierman,
Editor, *L.A. Parent* magazine

About the author:

Dorothy Jordon has been involved with the travel industry for 26 years. She is the founder and managing director of TWYCH, Travel With Your Children, the resource information center for parents and travel agents on family travel.

Dorothy Jordon is the leading spokesperson in the nation on family travel. Since 1984 she has published **Family Travel Times®**, America's only newsletter specializing in family travel. She was the contributing travel editor to *Family Circle* and was the travel editor for *Child Magazine*. Her family travel columns and articles have been published in *Parents Magazine, USA Today, The New York Times, Ladies Home Journal, Travel Weekly, The Los Angeles Times, Diversion, Travel/Holiday magazine, Condé Nast Traveler* and more. She has appeared on national television's Good Morning America, Live with Regis and Kathy Lee, The Today Show, ABC's Business World, CBS News, FOX News, CNN, Financial News Network, The Travel Channel and many more programs.

Dorothy is married and lives in New York City with her husband and two sons. They all still enjoy family vacations together.

Here's to

Great Nature Vacations

With Your Kids!

Dorothy Jordon

by Dorothy Jordon

World Leisure Corporation
Hampstead, NH Boston, MA

Distributed to the trade in USA by
LPC Group, 1436 West Randolph Street,
Chicago, IL 60607; tel. (312) 733-8228; (800) 626-4330

Distributed to the trade in Canada by
E.A. Milley Enterprises, Inc., Locust Hill,
Ontario LOH 1J0, Canada; tel. (800) 399-6858.

Distributed to the trade in the U.K. by
Roger Lascelles,
47 York Road, Brentford, Middlesex TW8 0QP; tel. 081-847-0935.

Mail Order, Catalog and Special Sales by
World Leisure Corporation, 177 Paris Street, Boston, MA 02128;
tel. (617) 569-1966 fax. (617) 561-7654

ISBN: 0-915009-47-1

This book is dedicated
To my father, Charles Jordon,
who instilled in me a lifelong love of travel

To my mother, Sydelle Jordon,
who taught me the everlasting importance of family

To David, Jordon and Russell Ferber,
my favorite travel companions and most ardent supporters.

ACKNOWLEDGEMENTS

Throughout this book I use the word "we" in lieu of "I." This is because this entire series could not have been created without the help and assistance of the many contributors to **Family Travel Times**®.

Specifically, I want to thank Joy Anderson for her patience and fine editing and writing skills. Special thanks are also due Debra Wishik Englander, Holly Reich, David I. Ferber, Ronnie Mae Weiss, Claudia Lapin, Carol Eannarino, Ann Banks and Candyce Stapen and the numerous other parents who shared their travel experiences with us.

No book of this sort can be complete without the participation of our "test" children—Jordon Ferber, Russell Ferber, Victoria Anderson, Rachel Shapiro, Kate Petre, Jenny Jordon, Alissa Kempler, Jonah Sobel, Daniel Sobel, Dylan Kreitman, Jenna Kreitman, Elise Englander and Adrienne Bernhardt.

I also would like to thank the many tour organizations, hoteliers, and public relations representatives who helped us gather the necessary details for this book.

Table of Contents

Great Nature Vacations

With Your Kids

INTRODUCTION

If you are one of today's traveling families looking for outdoor vacations in which both parents and kids come face-to-face with the natural world, this book is for you. Whether your children are babies, toddlers, school aged or teens, whether you're a member of a traditional two-parent family, a single parent, a grandparent, another relation or a member of a multigenerational group, **Great Nature Vacations With Your Kids** is certain to give you appealing and workable choices.

As editors of *Family Travel Times*, the newsletter devoted to making family vacations easier, more enjoyable and most rewarding, we have been writing about this genre of vacation since 1984. We know that today's generation of families is always seeking new and exciting travel ideas. Our goal, both in our newsletter and in this book, is to help your travel dreams become reality. As parents with extensive experience in the travel industry and seasoned travelers with our own children, we know first-hand that sharing nature with children can be wonderful and rewarding — though certainly not effortless. For *Great Nature Vacations With Your Kids*, we've done extensive research to determine what the best family nature experiences are, who operates the best programs for families and where you can easily find do-it-yourself possibilities. This information is combined with our tried-and-true advice.

WHAT IS A NATURE VACATION?

Simply defined, a nature vacation qualifies as any trip or expedition which ventures into areas where animals, birds, fish or plants can be found in their natural surroundings. It can be a spontaneous day trip, a weekend getaway, a sea voyage, a journey to exotic climes focusing on the environment, or a stay at a plush resort with a roster of nature-oriented expeditions nearby. Whatever you crave, the family-friendly possibilities are more numerous than ever before.

In this book, you'll find the opportunity to swim with dolphins, join a whale-watching excursion, hike a rain forest, check out bird populations from a variety of vantage points, and many more mind-boggling choices. Regardless of the ages of your children, we guarantee that there are myriad choices for you within these pages.

You may opt for a *Toddler Tromp* with the Appalachian Mountain Club in New Hampshire; select a *Family Dino Dig* in Colorado; head for the clear turquoise waters of Cancun, Mexico, and visit the Sian Ka'an Biosphere while luxuriating at a five star resort; or choose to sleep under the stars while you learn about the outdoors on a *Family Camping* trip with the Chewonki Foundation in Maine.

It's not necessary to join an organized excursion. Many hotels, resorts and inns extend warm welcomes to young guests and provide numerous on-site nature activities. Choose a condo or a deluxe hotel at Colorado's Keystone Resort, ensconce yourself in a cabin on Lake Champlain while visiting The Tyler Place in Vermont or choose a cabin only accessible by boat at Ludlow's Island Resort in Minnesota. The options we share with you in this book run the gamut — from roughing it to living it up in the lap of luxury.

You may select a journey we think of as a "no-brainer" — in which every day is organized for you — or plan a trip in which you pick and choose your outings on a daily basis, combining outdoor experiences with other forms of relaxation. For families with divergent interests, there are getaways which satisfy everyone, e.g., dad and daughter go off on a canoe trip while mom heads for a spa and the teenager signs on for a tennis clinic.

We know, from our many years of experience, that there are many possible and probable combinations on a family vacation. We also recognize that each family has different needs at different times. Our own children are now teenagers and we've traveled with them from when they were very small to now, when they're bigger than we are. We must be doing something right, since our teens are still anxious to travel with us. Yes, we do plan our vacations very differently now than we did when our kids were babies and toddlers. But, most importantly, we have consistently taken the types of vacations we wanted to take — with our kids — and have come home feeling relaxed, knowing that we did the right thing by taking our children with us. In fact, hindsight tells us that we gained much more from our journeys than we would have had we left the kids at home. We have had the opportunity to see the world through their eyes and, perhaps more importantly, to discover the beauty and secrets of our world side-by-side with them.

Nature-oriented trips (sometimes called green travel or ecotourism) have a dimension beyond the delight of coming into touch with the natural world. Most providers of this genre of travel encourage participants to become environmentally responsible travelers.

When this book series was in development, we intended to call this a guide to ecotourism for families, but soon decided that the term "ecotourism" is an oxymoron. Tourism, by its very nature, impacts negatively, not positively, on the environment, despite the best efforts of tour organizers and tourists.

By way of example, let us share an incident which occurred in the rain forest in Costa Rica on the final day of a Temptress Voyage (see page 96) last summer. It was incredibly exhilarating to come upon a large troupe of howler monkeys frolicking in the trees above us. Our small group had anxiously looked for these critters all week long. Though we tried to remain quiet, the monkeys realized that we were there, and seemed to become angry. They started throwing small branches at us, basically telling us to *"GO AWAY."*

At the time, this episode intimidated us only slightly but reflection has made us consider the effect tourists have on indigenous wildlife. So far, these animals' limited exposure to humans does not appear to have altered their lives dramatically, but one cannot help but feel that with the growing number of visitors, this will soon change. We believe that there is no better time for the would-be ecotourist to explore the world than right now.

HOW THIS BOOK IS ORGANIZED

We've divided this book into seven chapters. The first chapter examines the more practical angles of organizing a family nature trip while those that follow describe stimulating, intimate, first-hand encounters with nature.

Our listings are only the tip of the iceberg, so to speak. There are many, many more organizations out there that can help you and many of the resources we mention will be able to give you additional possibilities.

We haven't participated in each and every trip we describe, although we'd like to, but we have sampled quite a few with kids of all ages. We also have spoken with numerous other family participants. What struck us most about these trips was that we quickly developed appreciation for even those activities we didn't anticipate enjoying.

Birdwatching is a prime example. We know that it is considered America's second most popular hobby (the first being gardening), but the idea of taking a trip or a hike specifically to look at and identify these winged creatures held zero appeal for us adults — not to mention our kids. Yet, when we were out in a boat riding through an ancient Mayan canal in Mexico's Yucatan Peninsula and saw giant osprey, brightly colored cormorants and other birds, we actually became excited. The excitement built a few months later when we discovered that the huge nests we found in Jackson Hole, Wyoming, were the summer homes of the same osprey we observed in Mexico. "Our osprey," 14-year-old Russell exclaimed when he learned the news, feeling very proprietary.

Throughout this book you will see sidebars entitled *Booked for Travel*. These short book reviews cover a wide range of categories. There are books on specific types of activities, books with listings of invaluable resources, even books to read to and with your children to enhance your vacation experience. Some of the books will explore areas in your own backyard while others will take you to the far corners of the earth. Not all of them are specifically travel-oriented books, yet, in some way, each one could relate to your family's nature trip. We hope that these short book reviews entice you to set up your very own family nature library.

Our goal has been to find family-friendly trips, destinations and lodgings with nature activities that strike a balance of hands-on field trips, informative learning sessions and free time. No good nature encounter should make you feel like you've gone back to a dry-as-dust classroom of your youth. On the contrary, you should return every evening excited and invigorated by the day's activities. Don't try to do too much. Experience has taught us that traveling with children requires a certain amount of relaxation time built into each day. This is just as true when traveling with teens as it is when traveling with toddlers.

After the chapters, you'll find a series of appendices — Best For Babies, Toddlers, Teens, Multigenerational Groups, etc. Even though each listing delineates the ages that its programs are most appropriate for, you may decide to check out these appendices first.

BOOKED FOR TRAVEL

The Green Travel Sourcebook: *A Guide for the Physically Active, the Intellectually Curious, or the Socially Aware,* by Daniel and Sally Wiener Grotta, receives accolades from no less an authority than Sir Edmund Hillary, the conqueror of Mt. Everest. In his opinion, this is, "An amazing book . . . for the increasing number of us who want to dare a little — to breathe fresh air and sweet smelling flowers." The book addresses the question of green travel opportunities for families in the first few pages. The advice is simple — know your child's capabilities, take time to include him in the planning process, prepare him for the trip in advance and ask the right questions of the tour operator before booking. A long list of tour operators is provided. As you review the lists of trips, those suitable for kids will be apparent. (John Wiley)

CHAPTER 1: Planning Your Family Nature Vacation: How to choose a vacation, know which questions to ask, prepare your kids, avoid the pitfalls, make memories — in short, all the tools you need to make your vacation happen.

CHAPTER 2: Educational Organizations: Many of the premier associations with a scientific and/or educational commitment to our natural world offer all sorts of opportunities for family travelers.

CHAPTER 3: Tour Operators & Specialized Travel Services: All the tour operators in this chapter have had experience working with families — and understand the differences between the travel needs of children and adults.

CHAPTER 4: On the Water: There's no better vantage point from which to view a wide variety of creatures and explore shorelines than from a boat.

CHAPTER 5: Destinations: Not everyone is interested in an organized trip, especially one that requires constant packing and unpacking. At our destinations, your family can settle in for as long as you like, enjoy the day-trip opportunities we highlight, and return each night to the comforts of home.

CHAPTER 6: Stay & Play: This section is ideal for those seeking a comfortable lodging experience in combination with daily outdoor excursions organized by an on-site staff. Some properties offer childcare for infants, others sponsor teen programs. All aim to please families.

CHAPTER 7: Animal Encounters & Day Trips: Readers with little time should check out our numerous day trip choices.

We've deliberately omitted the obvious from this book. There's little mention of national parks (since so much has already been written about them) and few details on the vast system of state parks. Also, with the exception of organized camping trips, information on campgrounds is not included within these pages. Families who enjoy camping should contact Go Camping America at 800-47-SUNNY and ask for free camping vacation planners.

Bear in mind that our state parks, perhaps the best travel bargains available in the United States today, generally offer budget-priced accommodations and activities along with first-class and richly-varied scenery. Enjoy the wildlife, explore the walking trails and participate in the available nature, children's or family programs. Because they're such good deals, accommodations, including the campgrounds, are often booked well in advance, sometimes as far as a year ahead. Some examples of family activities in state parks can be found in Chapter 7.

While **Great Nature Vacations With Your Kids** covers trips to a number of foreign countries, most of our suggested do-it-yourself possibilities are set in North America, since we anticipate that the majority of you reside on this continent. From the Rocky Mountains to the California Desert, the lakes of Minnesota to the barrier islands of Florida, the rain forests of Costa Rica to the Caribbean's awesome reefs, the rivers of Idaho to the swamps of the Southeast — this book will have your family packing its bags.

BOOKED FOR TRAVEL

Among the best books for information on state parks are: **State Parks of the Midwest—America's Heartland:** *A Guide to Camping Fishing, Hiking & Sightseeing* by Vici DeHaan (Johnson Books); **The Best Bargain Family Vacations in the U.S.A.** by Laura Sutherland & Valerie

Deutsch (St. Martin's Press); **Plan-It, Pack-It, Go:** *Great Places to Tent; Fun Things to Do* (Woodall); **Campground Directory,** (Woodall, North America version, Eastern or Western US; 8 regional editions); **Camper's Guide to . . .** *Where to Go, How to Get There,* by Mickey Little (Gulf Publishing, various regions).

Additionally, this is the first of our **Great Vacations With Your Kids** series. The guide, **Great Adventure Vacations With Your Kids**, focuses on the physically active aspects of outdoor vacations: biking, hiking, camping, canoeing, covered wagon trips, dogsledding, mountain biking, rafting, rock climbing and more. We've tried to avoid overlap between the two books, so if you don't find what you're looking for here, turn to the *Adventure* volume for yet more options.

Other books in the series you can look forward to are: **Great Cruising Vacations With Your Kids, Great Sports Vacations With Your Kids, Great Island Vacations With Your Kids** and **Great Learning Vacations With Your Kids**. We believe that each and every one of these books will open the door to many fun and exciting family vacations.

Of one thing we're convinced: there are wonderful times in store for your family — wherever you may roam.

CHAPTER 1

PLANNING YOUR FAMILY NATURE VACATION

The Green Travel Sourcebook says that children are "the original Green Travelers, because everything is new and possible to them and because their minds and spirits haven't yet been shackled by adult-hood limitations." Moreover, the authors add, the best reason to take the kids on any kind of family trip is because "it adds to the fun." We couldn't agree more.

Time together as a family is precious time. Magical moments occur when parents and children share experiences which open up one's curiosity about the world around us. Our children will inherit the earth in the way in which we leave it. The more knowledge we impart to them in their childhood, the more they experience and the more they see, the more likely they will be open to making the necessary changes to ensure a better future for their own children.

When children learn first-hand what actually happens to lands that have lost all of their trees, they may better understand the need to replant and recycle. Once youngsters see wildlife in native habitats, they understand the need to upgrade zoo facilities to provide a more benign environment for animals. After a child's very first snorkeling expedition or scuba dive, a trip to your local aquarium takes on new meaning.

When our children were too young to snorkel we took dry, sugarless cereal to the beach and the fish came up to us, eating right out of our hands. Next we tried glass-bottom boat rides to view the ocean life below. Then we took an Atlantis Submarine (see page 188) which brought us deeper under the sea to places where only scuba-divers venture. Soon, every time we passed a fish tank, our boys tried to determine if the fish on display lived in the oceans we'd visited.

There are no limits to the mind-broadening effects nature trips will have on your children — and you. Experiencing a different milieu, as opposed to reading about it, takes us outside of ourselves, allowing us to see each other and the world around us in a new light.

Our best advice when selecting a nature outing holds true for all other family vacations: Choose a destination that you look forward to investigating as much as your children do. Don't be martyrs. After all, your children probably get up to 12 weeks of vacation each year — more than any adult is likely to have. Don't waste your precious leisure time taking your kids somewhere you think that they will like but one that you secretly dread visiting. Remember, kids often pick up your mood.

In the following pages, we've included vacations which appeal to the rugged as well as to the more sedentary among us. Some cost a lot; others are quite inexpensive. Some take you thousands of miles away from home; others only an hour or two away. Some are study trips while others are purely recreational.

BOOKED FOR TRAVEL

Whether you travel by plane, train or automobile, **We're Going on a Trip** will clue your children between the ages of 3 and 7 in on what kinds of experiences are in store for them. Parents will benefit from the extensive travel experience of author Christine Loomis, Travel Editor of *Family Life* and mother of three. The book includes advice on planning, packing and how to help things go smoothly once you're on the way. Maxie Chambliss's illustrations evoke an upbeat mood and reinforce the positive aspects of travel. (Morrow)

We firmly believe that no family trip need be labeled "educa- tional" since we consider that travel is intrinsically educational. Kids can't help but form new impressions while traveling. Though very young children may return with little to show for a family trip outwardly, a seed will have been planted in their minds. You may only discover what your older child has learned when you hear him or her conversing with a friend. Perhaps your children will return from a journey eating new, different foods; maybe they'll realize that not everyone in the world speaks English; possibly they'll note stronger cultural differences, as three-year-old Russell did after his first trip to Europe. When presented with a cold sandwich at lunch he insisted that if we were still abroad, his meal would have been warm. "Don't you know they eat their dinner at lunch?" he asked. Trust us, as children grow and mature, even when they don't specifically mention the cultural diversity they've seen, they will be gathering basic tools for becoming life-long travelers.

At the same time, we're not naive. We know that any family vacation, even an outdoors, nature-oriented one, is not going to be all fun and games and laughter every minute. Nonetheless, the collective memories of a vacation together are very special for each family member — and will last long after everyone has returned home.

PLANNING WITH YOUR FAMILY IN MIND

We venture to say that it's rare for all three, four, five or six members of your family to be together at once. We all experience those wild mornings when everyone's running off to school, to work or to the babysitter. Come evening, everyone is getting dinner together, running to meetings or organizing homework. These are the routines of everyday family life.

When we step out on vacation, we leave this hectic scheduling behind, granting us the time to hear what our children are saying and to take part in family conversations uninterrupted by the telephone. Best of all, we gain the added advantage of seeing the world through the perspective of our kids. More and more we have learned how traveling with our children leads us to new and unexpected encounters.

While all this togetherness provides for special family moments, the elusive "quality time" that people talk about, spending 24 hours a day hip-to-hip with our kids does not a vacation make — for us or them. Therefore, throughout this book we've tried to target tour operators, outfitters, resorts and destinations which offer our children the opportunity to meet and play with other youngsters while also giving us adults time away from parenting — something we believe should be part of any vacation experience.

We are raising the most highly socialized group of youngsters America has ever seen, youngsters who tend to thrive among their peers. Most will want to find other children to connect with, even when on holiday.

If your family is one that always wants to play together, there's no obligation to avail yourself of these services. For you, the advantages include having family amenities readily at hand, not to mention a child-friendly staff which will know how to service your needs and answer all of your questions.

It's obvious that organizing vacations with kids requires different strategies than going it alone. The entire vacation-planning process changed when you became part of a couple, and was further complicated when you included children and possibly grandparents. The key, of course, is setting a course that will pique everyone's interest and meet individual needs.

First, decide what *you'd* like to do. This is not an area in which to compromise. Where you go and stay may, in some way, be dictated by the ages and desires of your group, but the basic type of trip should not have to change.

Then, start with your youngest (if you're planning for a multi-generational group, start with the oldest and youngest and work your way towards the center), and make a list of physical needs. Are early dining times necessary? Will long hikes every day be too much? Should you bring a backpack?

Next, evaluate the maturity and flexibility of your kids. How well do they deal with groups? How do they cope with the unexpected? Try not to underestimate the capability of your children. We once spoke with a reader of our newsletter who participated in a llama trek with Steve Crone at Maine's Telemark Inn (see page 148). "I can't get my kids to walk to the mailbox, yet he was able to get them to hike more than five miles each day," she exclaimed. If you are uncertain, speak directly with the outfitters or trip organizer.

How about you? Are you a single parent who doesn't want to join a group of more traditional families? Are you nervous about water supplies or other health concerns? Don't hesitate to voice your concerns to the organization or tour you anticipate joining.

Last, set realistic expectations and avoid situations which might cause a conflict. As an example, suppose you've taken your child on her first camping trip. You've neglected to explain that the toilet facilities are different in the woods than they are at home. She may need to go to an out-building; there might be a "bathroom" set up for participants; she might be expected to use the woods. Feeling uncomfortable, and possibly even frightened, she becomes cantankerous and unmanageable rather than verbalizing her concerns. A few words of explanation in advance could have eliminated this problem.

We can't emphasize enough that communication with your kids about what to expect is of major import when you head for the great outdoors (or anywhere else). From trips with our own kids we've learned that the more your kids know, the easier and more carefree the adventure will be for everyone.

Real life is not *The Cosby Show*, so be wary not to set yourself up for disappointment. Something is going to go wrong, but if you're not expecting perfection, you're more likely to go with the flow and get through sticky situations easily.

Choose carefully and, remember —

It's not how much you do, but how much you enjoy doing it.

QUESTIONS TO ASK

With so many tour operators out there, how can you determine which one will provide your family with the best possible experience? Here are some questions that should help. Be certain that your questions relate directly to your specific needs.

- How long have they been offering tours which welcome children?
- Do the operators have children themselves?
- Describe the makeup of your group. Many of these trips are ideally suited to single parents with kids and other non-traditional configurations.
- If you join an organized tour specifically aimed at families, ask how it's different from other tours. Are there any special activities organized just for the kids?
- To what age group is the experience best suited?
- How large a group will you be joining?
- Exactly what is and isn't included in the cost?

- Is child-sized equipment provided? (On a side trip we took in Cancun, Mexico, there was time to snorkel off the side of the boat but, alas, no equipment for kids). If not, bring the necessary gear with you.

- What can they do if your child's a picky eater?

- How many naturalists and/or guides accompany the group? Are any of these parents, or do they have experience dealing with children?

- Are activities open to both parents and children?

- Where will you spend your nights?

- What facilities (toilet, shower, etc.), if any, are there?

- What are the emergency procedures in case of illness?

- Will they give you a reference? (Ask to speak with a family whose children are about the same ages as your own.)

Once you've gone through your list of queries, you may discover that one outfitter gave you a specific detail or some advice you want to go back and ask others about. Though this may result in extra work, it's worth it.

BOOKED FOR TRAVEL

Family Travel: *Terrific New Vacations for Today's Families*, by Evelyn Kaye, gives a nice overview of various non-traditional family vacation possibilities, e.g., eco-travel, volunteer vacations, home exchanges, farm stays and more. Her advice on planning is sound and though she lists a goodly number of destinations, organizations, etc., we would have liked to see many more, especially for the hefty $19.95 cover price. (Blue Penguin)

FINALIZING YOUR PLANS

Making the final decision about where to go and with whom may be your ultimate challenge. Organize those choices that fit the profile of your family and your budget. Your choice may be driven by the nature of the activities, the destination or even by the comfort level you anticipate experiencing.

Do include your children in the process. Have a family meeting and list the options. You may learn that there is a destination they've always dreamed of going to on your list. Conversely, you may learn that they dread a place you consider a definite possibility. You may be able to sway your kids to your point of view or perhaps they'll sell you theirs.

In the end, it's the parents who decide where and when families travel. Yet, nothing empowers children more than feeling they have control over their lives. When they have been consulted, their entire outlook toward the trip changes, both before and during the vacation, and the help you can expect from them to make things go smoothly greatly increases.

INVOLVING YOUR KIDS

As parents, for years we have been told that children thrive on knowing what to expect and knowing what's expected. When we take our kids on vacation, we throw this stricture to the wind and it is our job to replace it. The changes which are inherent in travel can be disorienting and upsetting to youngsters. When kids are involved in the vacation from the very beginning, much of this anxiety is eliminated. Walk through the entire trip with them, beginning with your mode of transportation, continuing with what you expect to see and do, where you'll sleep, who you might meet, and so on. Try and elicit some of their concerns and clear up any apprehensions. Share brochures and other travel literature with them. Give them lots of opportunity to ask questions. Always try and talk to them in terms they can relate to. Your child's teacher may prove to be a terrific resource in this regard.

Before You Leave Home

Getting kids excited for a trip is simple and books are the obvious starting point to pique their interest. When kids are young, find stories that tie in with your destination or type of trip you've planned. If you can find one with a character they already know, such as *Amelia Bedelia Goes Camping* for ages 6 to 10 or *Amos Goes Camping* for ages 3 to 5, all the better. An alphabet book which focuses on animals is ideal for a pre-schooler.

There are also travel guides written for children. Though the majority of the books in the **Kidding Around** series from John Muir

Publications feature city destinations, both the one on *Hawaii* and on *National Parks of the Southwest* take in sights you're likely to visit during your journey. Because they (like the **Taking the Kids** series from HarperCollins West) are written from a child's point of view, and use language kids can relate to (awesome is a favorite word), they are sure-fire kid-pleasers. Both of these series are suitable for children ages 8 and older who are competent readers.

When kids visit Hawaii they'll be on the lookout for surfers and hula dancers, whales and dolphins and volcanos and waterfalls. **Kidding Around: *The Hawaiian Islands*,** by Sarah Lovett, is the book that will help them track down their dreams. As they turn the pages, they'll learn plenty more — common Hawaiian words, folklore and legends, as well as down-to-earth important stuff like where to find the best beaches and the tastiest treats. Not only is this an entertaining work, it's the only guidebook to Hawaii aimed at children. (John Muir)

Older kids and parents can enjoy thumbing through guidebooks and ferreting out the most intriguing places to visit. See if one of Chronicle's **Places to Go With Children** series (see page 177) or Globe Pequot's **Family Adventure Guides** (see page 184) covers the geographic area you intend to visit. Teenagers are sure to have their own points of view on what interests them.

The Seven Natural Wonders of the World is sure to grab the interest of anyone who likes lists of the best, the most, etc. — as most children do! There's just the right amount of information about each place listed to keep kids interested. Since it's also a pop-up picture book, it's a pleasant way to introduce little kids to the concept of world geography. What are the seven natural wonders of the world? Author Celia King has tactfully named an example from each continent except Antarctica: the Great Barrier Reef, the caves of France and Spain, the harbor at Rio de Janeiro, the Paricutin Volcano in Mexico, the Grand Canyon, Victoria Falls, and Mount Everest. (Chronicle)

Beyond Books

Videos and TV can be counted on to grab a young person's attention. In addition to commercial travelogues, The Travel, Learning and Discovery Channels feature worthwhile and interesting programming. If you have a computer (and we know how much kids love computers), there are more possibilities — playing geography games, using travel-planning software, not to mention cruising the information super highway.

If you're traveling by car, make a map your first tool and let the kids help chart the route. Before you leave, mark off all of the sights everyone wants to see (you might even use different colors for each family member). Hopefully, by the time your children reach their teens, they will have acquired confidence and pleasure in their map reading and navigational skills through years of experience and they'll automatically feel in charge of shaping the vacation.

If you're headed to an exotic land, find it on a map or globe. Don't forget to talk about differences in time zones, climates and the like. You will find that this background information will also come in handy when you solicit the kids' assistance in packing for your journey, something we greatly encourage you to do.

BOOKED FOR TRAVEL

Maps and Mapping: *Geography Facts and Experiments* by **Barbara Taylor is part of the** *Young Discoverers* series. Not only will school-age children learn the many facets of classic cartography, the subject will come alive for them as they conduct their own experiments at home and in the field. (Kingfisher)

While On The Trip

One of the nicest features of joining an organized group is that the operator, not you, sets the rules so you can relax and enjoy yourselves. Be certain to set aside time each day for your family to share your collective experiences. Though we really like it when there are lots of other kids for our children to connect with, and appreciate the time organized children's activities provides for us adults, we also sometimes find that there's just not enough family together time, especially as our kids get older and their need to socialize (or sleep) dominates the available free time.

We highly recommend trying to record the magic of your trip for you and your children to relive years later. Should your children resist the suggestion of writing in a journal each day, be creative. If you've come face-to-face with newborn baby seals out on the ice floes of Quebec's Gulf of St. Lawrence on Natural Habitat Adventures' *Seal Watch* (see page 65), take a photograph or draw pictures together later in the day. If you spend a day collecting shells on a beach, make a craft item with them either that day or at home.

No matter how rich and fascinating a trip turns out to be, it's not possible to remember everything that went on. The old standbys really work — writing postcards to yourself which can later be kept in a scrapbook, making collections of found objects or souvenirs and the like, and taking photos at every turn.

BOOKED FOR TRAVEL

We've come across three travel journals for children that we can recommend. **Children's Travel Journal**, by Ann Banks, is our favorite. We like every single thing about it, especially Adrienne Hartman's charming and clever pen and ink drawings. This is a good choice if you're traveling overseas since there are world maps for charting an itinerary and pages on which kids can fill in information about passports, immigration and customs, and language and foreign money. (Little Bookroom, 212-691- 3321) . . . Our 11-year-old daughter preferred **My Vacation Book: For Kids By Kids**, by the Ilse children, Kellan, 10, and Trevor, 8. She felt that since it was written by children, its perception of what's fun and interesting to children was more valid. It includes travel games, number fun, cool sights, pockets for vacation memorabilia and plenty of blank pages for dood-ling. The focus here is domestic, with a map of the states and activities relating to U.S. license plates. (Wintergreen) . . . **Memories From Vacations Past** comes in a large, loose-leaf binder format, with a striking cover adorned with classic travel decals. Multiple journal entries, drawing paper, scrapbook pages with mounting stickers and album pages for photos are provided — so that the book can be used for a number of trips. There are ziplock pouches for unmountable keepsakes and a marker. The publishers urge the whole family to get involved in recording vacation reminiscences; we couldn't agree more! (Jamsco)

Memories can be kept alive by talking among yourselves, reminiscing, comparing notes and writing down each person's impressions. We've heard of families who take along a tape recorder and make "sightseeing" tapes on which both parents and kids describe what they're looking at. Listening to these tapes months or years later brings back fond remembrances.

BOOKED FOR TRAVEL

First Photos: *How Kids Can Take Great Pictures*, by Art Evans, should interest any child age 7 or older. The premise is that children can learn the basics of composition, the importance of light, how to choose an interesting subject, etc., and come up with excellent results using a disposable, inexpensive camera. The photos themselves speak volumes. For travelers, there are chapters on vacation snapshots and albums. We give it an A+. (Photo Data Research, 310-543-1085)

As you read the following pages, we hope you become as excited about the range of possibilities as we are. Try to be open-minded; we freely admit that we weren't initially turned on by some of the activities we now highlight. Searching for shells along a beach was far less meaningful before we learned where, why and how shells reach the shore. We were appalled at the idea of awakening daily at 6:30 a.m. on vacation to go hiking in Costa Rica, but became so energized and invigorated by our encounters that we actually made the effort to wake up even earlier to catch a sunrise.

Wonderful experiences await you and your family out there in the natural world. So, sit back and relax and read about the myriad possibilities we've explored.

CHAPTER 2

EDUCATIONAL ORGANIZATIONS

The listings which follow include tours run by museums, preservation societies and other non-profit associations that have spent years sharing the magic of the wilderness with tourists. On these organized trips (as on most of the trips featured in this book) an expert naturalist, one with experience in relating to children of various ages, is on hand to share his/her vast stores of knowledge. The fact that these groups all have lofty and serious aspirations in no way minimizes the fun you'll experience on their excursions. On the contrary — their enthusiasm is quite infectious.

Each listing contains a *PROFILE* of the organization, a description of the *PROGRAMS* it offers to families, sample *PRICES* and whom the trips are *PRIMARILY FOR*. All of the age limitations are offered as guidelines. There is often no exact minimum age, unless insurance policies impose strict age restrictions. If you're uncertain whether or not a trip is appropriate for your family, call the company and describe your child and his/her experience and capabilities.

In a recent conversation with Alana Hayman of Born Free Safaris (see page 55), we asked about the minimum age for a specific trip. Immediately we knew that she was tuned in to families. "I'd have to speak with the family," she said. "We've taken children as young as 2 who have fared beautifully, while some 5-year-olds have found the journey too rigorous."

Don't hesitate to ask if a program can be customized for your family when your children do not meet the specific age requirements of a group tour. Personally, we feel that our kids enjoy trips more when there are other children on the journey, so consider putting together your own small group of families.

APPALACHIAN MOUNTAIN CLUB (AMC)
5 Joy Street
Boston, MA 02108
Phone: 617-523-0636
Fax: 603-466-3871

PROFILE: AMC is a membership organization that is heralded as the oldest conservation and recreation association in America. It believes that "Responsible recreation ... depends upon first-hand enjoyment of the natural environment." Its flyer, *Family Adventure Club—An AMC Guide to Hiking With Children*, is one way it encourages families to take part in this enjoyment. Several AMC series of guidebooks, including one aimed at families, are published by the organization.

AMC operates a number of moderately-priced lodges, camps and huts that are open to members and non-members alike. Among them are the Joe Dodge Lodge at Pinkham Notch, Bascom Lodge, Crawford Hostel and several campgrounds. Year-round, a number of multi-day educational workshops are offered at facilities located in the White Mountains of New Hampshire, New York's Catskill Mountains, the Berkshires of Massachusetts and Maine's Acadia National Park, several of which are specifically designed for children and their parents and/or grandparents. Additionally, day-long programs are offered at the Pinkham Notch Visitor Center (New Hampshire), Crawford Hostel (New Hampshire) and Bascom Lodge (Massachusetts).

During the summer months activities focus on hiking and forest explorations. In winter, the emphasis is on backcountry skiing, snowshoe tours, dogsledding and more. Interpretive programs for all ages are on hand at all of the facilities.

PROGRAMS: During the spring and summer months, seven *Family Focus* weekends are held in the White Mountains, one in the Berkshires and three in the Catskills. They include *Family Discovery Weekends*, each with a specific nature focus (e.g., wildflowers, weather, birding, nature crafts, etc.) for children of all ages, *Curious Explorers for Preschoolers* and *Grandparent/Grandchild Nature Weekends*. Elderhostel (see page 31) also runs a five-night intergenerational course.

What can you expect? Well, during one of the *Curious Explorers Weekends,* featured activities included *Forest Foray,* a short hike checking out the local animals and plants. After lunch back at the Lodge, a mural, aptly called *Woodland Artists,* was created from the objects discovered on the morning excursion. This was followed by a rehearsal and costume-making session for an early evening performance of *The Grandpa Tree* and a talk on *Bear Habits and Habitats.* The next day the focus was on water, with stream-based activities and a pond study. Throughout the family sessions, snacks energized the body and games and songs kept minds alert.

There are a number of workshops which are appropriate only for adults. If you want to enroll in one of these, and still bring along your kids, ask for dates of the day camps in the White Mountains, which are held at various times in July and August for ages 7 to 9 and 10 to 12.

From early July through Labor Day, one-week *Family Camps* take place at *Echo Lake Camp* on Mount Desert Island, the home of Acadia National Park, in Maine. These camps fill up early and require reservation requests no later than April 1, after which spaces are assigned by lottery. Best for children about 5 years and older, AMC sponsors many nature activities, but none specifically for kids. There are, however, park ranger children's programs in Acadia National Park. Close friends of ours participated in a *Family Camp* last season when their children were 6 and 9 years old. They loved it and are anxious to return again this year.

In addition to these outings, family programs are also operated by individual chapters, such as the Boston Chapter's *Family Camping on Martha's Vineyard.*

PRICES: Family membership is $65/year. Benefits include discounts on workshops (some are exclusively for members) and lodging, plus a subscription to *AMC Outdoors* magazine. Programs and lodging are moderately priced. The *Curious Explorer Weekend* costs about $100/adult, $50/child. Weekly *Family Camp* prices for non-members are $344/adult, $296/ages 11 to 15, $213/ages 4 to 10. Prices are generally 10 percent less for members.

PRIMARILY FOR: All ages. Toddlers, teens, single parents and grandparents will find an exciting program to join.

We were so pleasantly surprised by the amount of thought and space given to children in **Nature Hikes in the White Mountains**. The author, Robert Buchsbaum, clearly supports taking your kids out on the trails — and gives you the tools with which to decide which jaunts will be the most successful. Moreover, he highlights all kinds of activities kids will like and provides thoughtful caveats for parents. The section on flora and fauna should definitely be read in advance as it's sure to pique your children's interest and give them items to seek out on the trail. A real winner of a book, this easily could have been entitled *Nature Hikes **With Kids** in the White Mountains*. (AMC Books)

CANYONLANDS FIELD INSTITUTE (CFI)
Box 68
Moab, UT 84532
Phone: 800-860-5262/801-259-7750
Fax: 801-259-2335

PROFILE: Founded in 1984, CFI's goal is to involve the average citizen in environmental and community issues. Focusing on the biology, geology and history of the Colorado Plateau of the Four Corners area (where Colorado, New Mexico, Utah and Arizona meet), CFI courses stress how recreational travelers can minimize their impact on the environment.

Westwater Canyon, nicknamed Little Grand Canyon, serves as CFI's base for many of its organized or customized trips. Here, you will be in close proximity to more than a thousand bald eagles now nesting nearby, glimpse mountain lions, big horned sheep, and so on.

Guests who participate in the day-long workshops must make their own lodging arrangements, though CFI can provide information on local options. If you have a group of 10 or more, ask about their Professor Valley Field Camp rental.

CFI's long-range plans include establishing a seminar site at a ranch-type setting in the Canyonlands region.

PROGRAMS: CFI's main commitment is to educating youth and, happily, it has expanded its options for kids while still operating a number of exciting trips which welcome parents and children. Among the latter is a one-day *Eagle Float* which takes place in March for children ages 6 and older. A three-day trip along the Colorado River, *Exploring Horsethief & Ruby Canyons*, is a calm water float also open to children ages 6 and older. *Exploring Westwater Canyon* is for more adventurous families with children at least 12 and older. This four-day trip winds down the river from Loma, Colorado to Cisco, Utah, and visits a variety of native Indian rock art and historical ruins. Elderhostel (see page 31) coordinates a number of trips with CFI: one of them, the *San Juan River Raft/Inflatable Kayak Trip*, is designed for grandparents with grandchildren between the ages of 8 and 14. It offers six Sunday to Friday summer departures.

CFI's one-day trips, which operate in the area of Moab, generally welcome kids 6 and older, as do many of the multi-day hiking and river trips which are not specifically designated as family trips. Half- and full-day adults-only courses, accompanied by experienced outdoor leaders, include hiking and studying local geological and cultural sites. Customized trips, for groups of eight or more, are always a possibility, as is the option for parents to take a day program while kids participate in CFI's day camps.

Geowhiz Kids for children ages 6 to 11 features four half-day outings, runs three times over the summer and costs $48. *Geowhiz Adventure* is aimed at children ages 12 to 15 with full-day outings over a five-day period for $90/child. Again, three summer sessions are offered. Advance registration is necessary. Each session will focus on a separate theme or adventure and is designed to increase both observational skills and appreciation and understanding of the natural world. The teen program concentrates on learning and adventure: hiking, rafting, canoeing and orienteering. Multi-day *Explorer Camps* for youngsters require reservations and include *Whitewater Academy for*

Teens (ages 13 to 18), *Paddling Labyrinth Canyon* (ages 14 to 18), *Paddling the Goosenecks* (ages 14 to 18) and *High Above and Deep Below* (ages 11 to 13). Check directly with CFI for dates and prices. The majority of these trips are frequented by local youngsters as opposed to tourists.

PRICES: All participants become "complimentary" members through May of the following year. However, a prepaid family membership of $35 entitles you to a discount of up to $15/person on programs, a newsletter and other discounts. Prices listed here do not reflect these discounts. The *Eagle Float* trip is $80/adult, $60/child under 18. *Exploring Horsethief & Ruby Canyons* is $330/adult, $265/child. *Elderhostel* (no member discounts offered) is $375/adult or child. Day trips are $50/adult, $35/child under 18.

PRIMARILY FOR: Children over 6, parents, grandparents and single parents. Each trip lists specific age recommendations.

THE CHEWONKI FOUNDATION
RR 2, Box 1200
Wiscasset, ME 04578
Phone: 207-882-7323
Fax: 207-882-4074

PROFILE: This non-profit educational foundation was formed in 1963 by the owners of Camp Chewonki, a boy's summer camp which dates back to 1915. Its long-standing mission is: "To foster personal growth through group interaction in the context of the natural world."

The area surrounding Chewonki's headquarters is incredibly rich in wildlife. Guests report regular sightings of moose, deer, loon and osprey. Courses, the majority of which are designed for families, encourage active participation: Expect to join in pitching tents, preparing meals, hoisting sails and the like.

Regardless of which trip you select, you're bound to find yourself face-to-face with nature's outdoor classroom, enjoying activities such as canoeing, camping or hiking. Though most courses take place in Maine, several venture as far afield as the Florida Everglades and Quebec, Canada.

PROGRAMS: On all of the family trips, you'll join a small group with a relaxed itinerary that allows time for each family member to receive instruction and practice newly acquired skills — not to mention have a good time. Three- to 10-day workshops and wilderness expeditions enhance one's appreciation of the natural world.

One of the courses which appeals to us the most is *Introduction to Canoe Camping*. This three-night trip, an ideal time frame for families, is held at an outpost on Wood Pond, a short paddle from the foundation's headquarters. Participants sleep in two platformed canvas yurts and cook over permanently installed wood stoves with propane lights. You'll learn how to handle a canoe, use camping gear, set up camp and become familiar with cooking over an open fire. There will be lots of time for swimming and exploring.

Another enticing trip is *Maine Coastal Sailing*. This week-long voyage takes place on a traditional wooden sailing boat which returns ashore each night for guests to camp in secluded coves. Need more choices? Ask about: *Sea Kayaking or Canoeing in the Florida Everglades; Coastal Sea Kayaking; Mountain Flowers of Katahdin; St. Croix River Canoe Trip; Moose River Camping* and more.

PRICES: Introduction to Canoe Camping costs $360/adult, $270/child 12 and under. *Coastal Sailing* costs $540/adult, $450/child.

PRIMARILY FOR: All configurations of family groups are welcome and encouraged. The minimum age for children is 8 on some trips, 10 and 14 on others.

COTTONWOOD GULCH FOUNDATION

October to May:	June to September:
P.O. Box 3915	P.O. Box 969
Albuquerque, NM 87190	Thoreau, NM 87323
Phone: 800-246-8735	Phone: 505-862-7503

PROFILE: Almost 70 years ago, the Cottonwood Gulch Foundation's *Prairie Trek and Turquoise Trail Expeditions* were created by educator Hillis Howe so youngsters could explore the Four Corners of Colorado, New Mexico, Arizona and Utah and use nature as an "outdoor laboratory." In recent years, a *Family Trek of Cottonwood Gulch* which explores remote regions of the Southwest and is limited to 25 participants, has been added.

PROGRAMS: Departing from Albuquerque, participants head for the hills in 15-passenger vans. They camp in tents and cook meals over an open fire. While this is not a rugged trip, you will find yourself roughing it. The base camp in the Zuni Mountains of western New Mexico has no electricity or running water. However, it does have a swimming pool and portable showers. The numerous activities include walking, learning about native crafts and astronomy, and more, including a two-day horse pack trip in the Gila Wilderness. One of the highlights is the two nights spent in Chaco Canyon. Among the unusual topography are the remnants of volcanic lava flows, cinder cones and ice caves.

PRICES: $750/adult, $550/child.

PRIMARILY FOR: The eight-day trip is designed for parents with children ages 6 to 16. All family configurations are welcomed.

DENVER MUSEUM OF NATURAL HISTORY
2001 Colorado Boulevard
Denver, CO 80205-5798
Phone: 303-370-6304
Fax: 303-331-6492

PROFILE: The Denver Museum of Natural History's travel programs include both a series of weekend outings and longer forays further afield, from the sidewalks of San Francisco to the rain forests of Belize. Itineraries are designed to "observe the natural and cultural world," and each trip draws upon the resources of the museum collections and the academic expertise of its staff. Unfortunately, many trips run during the school year. Those of you doing home teaching who can afford to take both the time and the money to travel abroad would find it beneficial to be put on the museum's trip mailing list.

Curiously, the museum's travel brochure does not always indicate which trips are particularly welcoming to and/or appropriate for families. When we speak to the museum staff, however, it is clear that the museum believes in the importance of families participating in the travel experiences it offers. Like many museum travel programs whose emphasis has rarely been on families, when the Denver Museum has tried to aim a specific trip exclusively at families, the response has been minimal. To rectify this, the museum is now encouraging families to join specific programs while continuing to create family trips.

PROGRAMS: One expedition that welcomes families is a March excursion to Belize. The nine-night trip explores rain forests, reefs and ruins, and appeals to snorkelers, divers and those with an interest in Mayan culture. Much of the focus is on the diversity of marine life and the rich flora and fauna of the rain forest.

It begins with a two-night stay at a working ranch, exploring the Macal River Valley while walking trails, swimming and canoeing. Then the group heads for Mountain Pine Ridge and a permanent tented camp for three nights, venturing into the Chiquibul Rainforest. Next the group visits the Belize Zoo and Tropical Education Center en route to Jaguar Reef Lodge for the last five nights. The tour also includes stops at the Cockscomb Basin Jaguar Preserve, searches for manatee in Anderson's Lagoon and snorkeling or diving among blue nose dolphin, sea turtles, golden-spotted morays and giant lettuce coral along the second largest barrier reef in the world.

Another trip which might be of interest to families, since it falls during a traditional school vacation week in February, is *Art and Archaeology of the Oaxaca Valley*, which studies the anthropology, archaeology and folk art of the region.

Jurassic Journey, the museum's latest "designed-for-family" program, has met with great success. The four-day, three-night trip includes a visit to the Dinosaur National Monument in Utah and rafting on the Green River.

Another "family program" heads for Chaco Canyon in New Mexico. *Archaeoastronomy of the Southwest* focuses on Anasazi culture and history and is accompanied by members of the International Association for Astronomical Studies (IASS), a group of junior and senior high school students taking part in a study under the direction of a staff member from the Gates Planetarium. The three-night camping trip activities feature "star parties," informal lectures and hands-on workshops.

PRICES: The trip to Belize, which includes round trip air fare from Denver, costs about $2,300/adult with a $300 discount for children under 12. *Jurassic Journey* costs $590/adult and $470/child 5 to 11. Accommodations for the first night are not covered in the cost. *Archaeoastronomy of the Southwest* costs $140/adult, $90/children 6 to 12 and does not include meals or camping gear.

PRIMARILY FOR: The Belizean trip is geared for children in fifth grade and up. The Oaxaca tip is open to children 13 and older. *Jurassic Park* is designed for families with children age 5 to 11; *Archaeoastronomy of the Southwest* is for children 6 to 12.

BOOKED FOR TRAVEL

Expanded and revised, **What's in the Deep?** *An Underwater Adventure for Children*, by photojournalists Alese and Morton Pechter, is a wonderful introduction to the undersea world. It is the story of two children who go reef snorkeling with their marine biologist cousin. The latest edition, with more information on underwater photography, pirates and deep sea diving, is sure to inspire kids ages 5 and older. (Acropolis)

DINAMATION INTERNATIONAL SOCIETY (DIS)
550 Crossroads Court
Fruita, CO 81521
Phone: 800-DIG DINO
Fax: 970-858-3532

PROFILE: DIS is a research-based organization which "promotes education, research and preservation in the biological, earth and physical sciences with an emphasis on dinosaur paleontology." DIS's travel programs for dinosaur enthusiasts — and what child isn't turned on by dinosaurs these days? — help put the close relationship between the geology of the earth and the study of dinosaurs into focus.

DIS's **Devils Canyon Science & Learning Center**, a multimedia facility located near the entrance to Colorado National Monument, should appeal to the entire family with its wide array of interactive exhibits. Here, you and your kids can visit with robotic dinosaurs and check out a paleontological laboratory.

Both the Learning Center's and the trips' activities are integrated with scientific discoveries, ranging from earthquake simulations to making comparisons of dinosaurs to living animals.

PROGRAMS: Among DIS's *Dinosaur Discovery Expeditions* is *Family Dino Camp,* designed for families with children ages 6 to 12. With seven departure dates offered between June and August, the customized hands-on educational and fun projects are integral to the program's continued success. While much of the time is spent together, adults will have the opportunity to work in a real quarry, while kids work in a simulated environment. A visit to *Bookcliff Exotic Animal Park*, hiking the *Trail Through Time* and unraveling a dinosaur murder mystery are just some of the highlights. These trips concentrate on the Mygatt-Moore Quarry excavation near Grand Junction in Colorado. A number of other trips welcome teenagers, such as *Colorado Canyons* and the *Colorado Advanced Expedition.*

PRICES: Cost of the five-day/four-night *Family Dino Camp* is $800/adult, $575/child.

PRIMARILY FOR: The Learning Center is most suitable for children ages 3 and older. *Family Dino Camp* has a minimum age of 6; other trips have minimum ages of either 13 or 16.

BOOKED FOR TRAVEL

Stolen Bones by Joan Carris is an engrossing, suspense-filled tale for middle readers. When young Alex Wright travels to Montana to assist his grandfather, the eminent "Dr. Dinosaur," he encounters not one, but two mysteries: disappearing fossils and resentment over his presence. Over the course of its 160 pages, children will learn a tremendous amount about what really goes on at a dinosaur dig. (Little, Brown)

Dinosaur Digs is sure to bring out the budding paleontologist in your family. Not only will you find a geographic listing of museums and parks where you can view, touch, dig for or study these fascinating creatures, the book also provides the how to do it and the when it's best, including tips that help, tools you'll need to provide and which organizations sponsor family programs. This compendium of *dinosources* make this book a valuable addition to any family travel library. (Country Roads Press)

DISCOVERY TOURS OF THE AMERICAN MUSEUM OF NATURAL HISTORY
Central Park West at 79th Street
New York, NY 10024-5192
Phone: 800-462-8687/212-769-5700
Fax: 212-769-5755

PROFILE: Since 1953, AMNH's Discovery Tours has sponsored trips exploring all parts of the globe, designed to "enhance your appreciation and understanding of the natural world." For a number of years it has offered family trips to such places as the Galapagos Islands, Africa and the Greek islands.

PROGRAMS: Wildlife of the Galapagos, A Family Adventure visits the fragile ecosystem of this fascinating archipelago, whose abundant animal life inspired Darwin. Located off the Ecuadorian coast, the entire area teems with wildlife, from seabirds and giant tortoises to colorful fish and blue-footed boobies. This trip visits the city of Quito, the Andean Highlands and 10 of the islands. You'll have chances to snorkel, watch Ecuadorian artisans at work, observe sinkholes, birdwatch and visit the Charles Darwin Research Center. Our experiences in the Galapagos with our own kids have been incredibly awe-inspiring, and so much fun, that we highly recommend this journey.

East Africa Safari is led by museum anthropologist Ann Prewitt. Your group (maximum 20) will explore some of the world's most awesome wildlife reserves (e.g., Nairobi National Park, Tarangire National Park, Ngorongoro Crater, Samburu Game Reserve, Maasai Mara), dine in a Kenyan home, visit a local school and meet African schoolchildren. Kids will love the stops at the Giraffe Center and the Langata Ostrich Farm, the game drive at Samburu and the numerous animals they'll encounter — from antelope to zebra.

PRICES: The 10-night *Galapagos* trip starts at $3,450/adult, $2,500/child ages 7 to 11 and $3,175/ages 12 to 15 and departs from Miami. Accommodations are on the MV *Santa Cruz*, a comfortable 90 passenger vessel that features both triple and quad cabins. The *Africa* trip, departing from New York, costs $5,680/adult, $4,573/child under 12 sharing with parents. There's a $650 single supplement. Land-only prices are about $1,400 less.

PRIMARILY FOR: Trips welcome children ages 7 and older. Multigenerational groups and single parents will be very comfortable as well.

ELDERHOSTEL
75 Federal Street
Boston, MA 02110-1941
Phone: 617-426-7788 - Administration
617-426-8056 - Registration
TDD: 617-426-5437

PROFILE: Elderhostel's series of learning adventures is aimed at adults ages 55 and older. Comprised of numerous short-term, inexpensive, academic-oriented programs, the courses take place across the country and around the globe. You may find yourself "on college and university campuses, in conference centers, in marine biology field stations and environmental study centers," enjoying "the cultural and recreational resources that go with them." For at least 10 years, *Intergenerational Courses* have been aimed at grandparents and their grandchildren. Throughout this book we've tried to pinpoint Elderhostel programs which correspond with our other write-ups, such as the one at the Appalachian Mountain Club (see page 20).

PROGRAMS: Intergenerational programs are specifically designed for the exchange between different age groups, where the joys of learning and discovery are shared by all — with kids-only/adult-only time also scheduled. Domestic programs are offered in more than 20 states and across Canada.

One example is the Sunday to Friday program at Otter Creek Park in Kentucky, 30 miles south of Louisville, set amid 3000 wooded acres rich in flora and fauna. Another is *Exploring Nature With Your Grandchildren* held at the Wolf Ridge Environmental Learning Center in Minnesota, overlooking Lake Superior. You'll be surrounded by maple forests and pristine lakes with numerous opportunities to view the abundant wildlife. There's even a program in Alaska, *Exploring Denali National Park: An Intergenerational Experience* which runs in June. Again, the program is tailored to meet the needs of the different age groups while aiming to enhance the very special relationship between grandparent and grandchild.

PRICES: *Otter Creek* costs $320/adult, $300/child; the six-night *Wolf Ridge* program is $345/adult, $245/child; *Denali* is $440/adult, $400/child. Children's prices (when they are different from adults) appear in the Elderhostel catalog — but only adults register through the Boston office. Once an adult is signed up, the child's booking is made directly with the appropriate facility. Adult prices include the $75 registration fee.

PRIMARILY FOR: Read the Elderhostel literature carefully to determine exactly what age children are accepted. As a general rule of thumb, children ages 8 and older are welcome, but often only one child per adult is allowed. We have noticed a few places which take children as young as 5, others where the minimum age is as high as 9 or 10. The Denali trip is specifically for children ages 10 and 11. Though most courses anticipate that the adult participants will be grandparents, many welcome older parents with children.

BOOKED FOR TRAVEL

The Seasoned Traveler: *Trips For Those With Time To Explore*, by Marcia Schnedler, is a book for older travelers. We've put it in a family-travel guide because intergenerational travel is becoming more common and because this volume offers a chapter *Going With Grandchildren*, listing organizations which cater to this niche. Moreover, Schnedler has a very upbeat, can-do approach to travel for healthy, active, older travelers. We like to think that we'll be globetrotting well into our golden years, and we'll feel doubly blessed if there are grandchildren to share our travels with. (Country Roads)

FAMILYHOSTEL OF THE UNIVERSITY OF NEW HAMPSHIRE
UNH Continuing Education
6 Garrison Avenue
Durham, NH 03824-3529
Phone: 800-733-9753/603-862-1147
Fax: 603-862-1113

PROFILE: Created in 1991, FAMILYHOSTEL caters to children, parents and grandparents interested in travel abroad with the intent to "learn about a foreign culture by living it!" It runs a series of 10-day trips in which participants stay in accommodations chosen because of their easy access to major attractions and nearby parks with playgrounds. Destinations for 1996 include: Prague, Vienna (these two can be combined), France (two trips), Wales and The Netherlands. In past years, Australia, Switzerland, Denmark and Mexico have been featured. These, and new locations, are rotated year to year. With the exception of the Australian tour, only one or two locations are visited on each trip. This leaves more time for the unique learning experiences they've organized and avoids the tedious task of frequent packing and unpacking during the trip. All of the programs feature activities for children, for adults and for families together. Pre-trip material includes reading recommendations for adults and kids, plus a scrapbook in which you are encouraged to create a lasting memory of your journey.

PROGRAMS: We'll cover FAMILYHOSTEL trips more in depth in our Learning volume, but we believe that you might enjoy the July journey to Wales, as it offers a number of excursions which fit into our nature category. Discover the red sandstone of Brecon Beacons National Park, a Welsh enclave of mountains and waterfalls. From Celtic history to ancient Roman and Norman traces, the trip includes a pony trek, a visit to the fortress and amphitheater at Caerleon, a canal boat ride and more. Past (and future) trips with a focus on nature explore Australia and Switzerland.

PRICES: *Wales: Abergavenny and Emlyn* costs $1,895/adult, $1,795/children 12 to 15, $1,595/children 8 to 11, and departs from New York. Land only prices are $1,343, $1,242 and $1,208 respectively. This particular trip has no single supplement, though others do.

PRIMARILY FOR: Recommended for children 8 to 15, though both older and younger children may be accommodated. Several of the trips have no single supplements, rendering them appealing to single parents and/or single grandparents.

BOOKED FOR TRAVEL

Getting kids interested and involved in your destination before a journey is one of the keys to a successful trip. **Cobblestone Publishing** has three top-notch magazines aimed at elementary and middle school children on topics that easily relate to travel.

Faces looks at countries and cultures with a broad overview of lifestyles, customs, religion, economics, government, hands-on activities for kids and a bibliography for further reading.

Calliope focuses on world history with sections on maps, time lines, word origins, archaeology and resource lists.

Odyssey introduces the wonders of science and technology on timely subjects, and often includes interviews with prominent thinkers on relevant topics. There are also projects and contests for children. *Odyssey's* volcano issue, for example, is great before a trip to Hawaii.

The best news is that you don't have to purchase a subscription to avail yourself of this unique educational opportunity. Call or write for their catalog; all issues are in stock. (Cobblestone Publishing, 7 School Street, Peterborough, NH 03458, 800-821-0115)

FRIENDS OF THE RIVER (FOR)
128 J Street
2nd Floor
Sacramento, CA 95814
Phone: 916-448-3820
Fax: 916-442-3396

PROFILE: Calling itself "California's leading river conservation organization," FOR works to protect and restore rivers in California. Recently, the organization obtained National Wild and Scenic Status for the Tuolumne, Kings, Upper Kern and Merced rivers thus preventing construction of a dam which would flood the canyon of the North and Middle Forks of the American River, home to diverse wildlife and plant habitats. Rich in threatened and endangered species, such as the peregrine falcon and bald eagle, the region encompasses spacious canyons plus almost 40 miles of whitewater boating which supports more than 30 outfitters.

Among the services FOR provides is information on various rivers and the outfitters that offer trips on them. FOR is happy to guide you toward the best possible experience for your family, but no longer makes the bookings. It will happily supply you with a list of family-friendly outfitters who support its conservation work.

PROGRAMS: FOR doesn't often sponsor trips, but it's always worth a call since many of its excursions are not planned far in advance. FOR is currently running a one-day trip to paddle down either the upper or lower stretches of the South Fork of the American River. This exciting trip, through some famous class III rapids, passes by spectacular scenery and includes lunch and the services of a certified guide.

PRICES: Membership is $40/family. The American River trip costs $75/person.

PRIMARILY FOR: There is a minimum age of 10 on the American River trip.

NATIONAL AUDUBON SOCIETY (NAS)
NAS Nature Odysseys
700 Broadway
New York, NY 10003
Phone: 212-979-3066
Fax: 212-353-0190

PROFILE: The mission of NAS Nature Odysseys is "to raise funds to conserve and restore natural ecosystems, focusing on birds and other wildlife, through education about and the enjoyment of nature by offering the finest natural history travel programs around the globe." NAS has established a stringent *Travel Ethic for Environmentally Responsible Travel* which is followed on all of their trips. Though NAS has been sponsoring trips since the 1950s, we were both surprised and quite pleased to discover that, though families are not the focus of these programs, children are neither unwelcome nor uncommon participants. Margaret Carnright, Director of Travel Programs, is a parent herself, and has a very clear understanding of how and why the trips are best suited to parents and children.

For information on NAS' non-travel-related fare, which includes adult workshops, separate youth and adult camps, and the 100 NAS owned and/or managed nature and wildlife sanctuaries, contact the head office at 613 Riversville Road, Greenwich, CT 06831 or call at 203-869-2017.

PROGRAMS: Originally designed as a family trip, *Impressions of a Swedish Summer* currently operates in late May/early June. Accompanied by expert birder John Borneman, the eight-day voyage journeys through the Swedish archipelago aboard the *Swedish Islander*, which carries its 49 guests in comfort and style. On board you'll find bicycles, fishing equipment (kids can ask the chef to prepare their catch) and Zodiac rafts for access to the more remote shores.

The trip begins with two nights at a charming hotel in the historic town of Soderkoping, from whence the Hansa League sailed in the Middle Ages. The first day is spent on the hotel's private boat, situated on the Gota Canal, sailing amid the St. Anna archipelago and visiting Eknon National Park. The next stop is an overnight stay in Trosa, the coastal town where the Swedish Islander is docked. Among the stops over the next four days are small islands off the beaten path that burst with vivid wildflowers, abundant wildlife and small towns which beg to be explored on foot or by bike.

Alaska Wildland Safari is a trip that often attracts teenagers with their parents or grandparents. However, NAS's top choice for families in Alaska is *Exploring Alaska's Coastal Wilderness*. Spot bald eagles, black bears, dolphins, whales and puffins during the week-long cruise aboard the MV *Sea Bird*, a shallow draft ship that allows for visits to sights inaccessible to larger vessels. Zodiac rafts are also on hand. As you cruise from Juneau to Sitka, daily naturalist-led excursions investigate the spectacular 20-mile-long Tracy Arm Fjord, tidepools and glaciers, the Tlingit Indian town of Haines, Glacier Bay National Park and Point Adolphus, a summer feeding area for humpback whales.

Among the Great Whales (in Baja, California, and the Sea of Cortez) sounds exciting and "terrific for families" as NAS claims, but departures are scheduled on dates when children are generally in school. Several Caribbean trips and travels through the Intercoastal Waterway are other options families might consider.

PRICES: *Impressions of a Swedish Summer* is $2,180/adult, $1,090/child under 16 sharing a room with two adults, $480/single supplement. *Alaska's Coastal Wilderness* costs from $2,990 to $4,190/person.

PRIMARILY FOR: Each trip has a designated minimum age, typically 8. *Swedish Summer* welcomes children 7 and older. Stiff single supplements make some of these trips expensive choices for single parents. Multi-generation groups are always popular. In Alaska, only three of the 36 cabins, which all have showers, can accommodate three passengers.

BOOKED FOR TRAVEL

Budding ornithologists who take the time to go step by step through Jorie Hunken's **Birdwatching for All Ages:** *Activities for Children and Adults*, will emerge as mini-experts in the field. A few of the subjects covered are how to: use binoculars, identify bird species, imitate bird calls, build birdhouses, draw birds, feed birds—the works. Kids will find the participation of an enthusiastic adult a big asset. (Globe Pequot)

NATIONAL WILDLIFE FEDERATION (NWF)
8925 Leesburg Pike
Vienna, VA 22184-0001
Phone: 800-245-5484/703-790-4363/800-822-9919-NatureLink
Fax: 703-790-4468

PROFILE: Founded in 1936, NWF offers the largest conservation education program in the United States. Best known to families for *Ranger Rick Magazine* and its renowned *Conservation Summits* and teen wildlife camps, its mission is to "inspire and assist individuals ... to conserve wildlife and other natural resources and to protect the earth's environment in order to achieve a peaceful, equitable and substantial future."

NWF now offers three options for families to explore our world: *Conservation Summits, NatureLink* and *Wildlife Weekends*. All of the destinations are chosen because of their natural beauty and for the ability of participants of various age groups and physical capabilities to get the most out of their visit.

PROGRAMS: *Conservation Summits*: In 1996 two summits will be held — Colorado Rockies at the YMCA of the Rockies in Estes Park and Alaska, in Seward and the Kenai Peninsula. These week-long encounters with nature offer more than 40 classes for adults to choose from and combine for a personalized learning experience. There are separate programs for children (child care for children under 3, half-day *Your Big Backyard* programs for children ages 3 to 5, full-day *Junior Naturalist* programs for children ages 5 to 8 and 9 to 12 plus *Teen Adventure* for those 13 to 17). From nature crafts and storytelling for the youngest, to outdoor leadership and problem solving skills for teens, the programs teach children about the "nature of tomorrow." Parental opinion on the programs is always laced with praise, particularly when describing the relationships between the naturalists and the kids.

Family-together choices, from bike rides or hikes to lecture/events such as *The True Wolf Story: Howls, Habits and Ecology, Observation Olympics: Games to Challenge Your Senses*, and so on are offered in the late afternoons, when the coursework is done.

Evening entertainment might include a square dance, songfest or more serious fare. Guests are also encouraged to take advantage of the many recreational facilities close by.

All NWF lodging options provide access to the outdoors, the basic comforts of home, good value and a meal plan alternative. Past *Summits* have taken place in Washington, North Carolina, Hawaii and California.

NatureLink: The goal of this weekend program is for families to reconnect with nature and the outdoors and, in doing so, acquire "a lifetime commitment to conservation." Programs are offered at a variety of destinations around the country and feature fishing, canoeing, wildlife identification and other nature-oriented events. In 1996, there will be 16 programs in 15 states. For families with limited time or money, this is a welcome opportunity. NWF can send you a 15- minute tape that is certain to tempt you to sign on. It worked on us!

Wildlife Weekends: This new-for-'96 program combines aspects of both of the above programs. Tentatively scheduled for late summer/early fall, these should especially appeal to those of you who don't have the time or dollars to participate in the full summits. As we go to print, particulars are not finalized.

PRICES: Fees for the *Summits* are $400/adult, $325/child 13 to 17, $300/child 5 to 12 and $175/child 3 to 4. Member discounts are about 20 percent. Lodging is additional and ranges from $400 to $800/adult and $150 to $400/child in Alaska, $350 to $600/adult, $108/child in Colorado. *NatureLink* weekends cost about $100/adult and $50/child. No prices are available for *Wildlife Weekends*.

NWF membership costs either $16 or $22/adult, $15/children 6 to 12. Call 800-588-1650 for explanations of benefits.

PRIMARILY FOR: Everyone is welcome to attend. More than 30,000 folks have participated in NWF programs, even those without children!

THE NATURE CONSERVANCY (TNC)
1815 North Lynn Street
Arlington, VA 22209
Phone: 703-841-5300
800-628-6860/703-841-4850 Member Services
Fax: 703-841-1283

PROFILE: The Nature Conservancy's mission is "To preserve plants, animals and natural communities that represent the diversity of life on Earth by protecting the lands and waters they need to survive." Founded in 1951 by members of a professional ecology association, TNC currently manages more than 1,500 preserves in the United States and works with like-minded organizations in Latin America, the Caribbean and the Pacific.

Information about this organization is not always easy to find until you become a member. Then you'll receive bi-monthly copies of their magazine, with listings of both regional and chapter programs and trips. Moreover, your local chapter will also continue to entice you with outings.

Excerpts from TNC's *Natural Events Almanac* can be found on America Online under *Nature Serve*. Want to see the migration of monarch butterflies? Head for Illinois' Cache River Joint Wetlands Project in late September. May and June is peak moose/wildlife viewing time at New Hampshire's Fourth Connecticut Lake Preserve. Sea turtles nest from May through August at Botany Bay Island in South Carolina while during June and July seal pups are born on the Yellow Island Preserve in Washington State. Bats return and reproduce in Eckert James River Bat Cave in Texas from late June through early July. These, and more, are among the items you're likely to learn about on-line.

PROGRAMS: Field trip listings in TNC's magazines rarely give any details on ages accepted, special prices for children or even suitability for families. Some exceptions: *Tensleep Family Adventures* are offered for your own group or for your family in conjunction with other families in Wyoming's Bighorn Mountains and are run by the Wyoming field office. Here are some of the highlights other chapters shared with us:

Kids are welcome on any of the Maryland chapter's local trips which include canoeing on Nassawango Creek at the Cypress Swamp Preserve and walking the 2,000-foot boardwalk at Choptank Wetlands Trail in Talbot County.

The Oregon chapter sponsors free day hikes that might include visits to Crater Lake, the Columbia River Gorge and other Pacific Northwest natural phenomena. There are also longer excursions in the region, e.g. *Llama Trekking in the Wallowa Mountains, Klamath Birding Weekends*, and further afield, e.g. *Exploring Southeast Alaska, Nature and the Maya in Belize and Tikal*. In all cases, the decision to bring children is left up to the parent.

The Kansas chapter invites you to visit Cheyenne Bottoms, a basin-like lowland area that is the largest system of wetlands in the state. During seasonal migrations, hundreds of thousands of shorebirds, wading birds and waterfowl stop to rest and feed here. The Nature Trail at Konza Prairie near Manhattan features a self-guided walking tour in its tallgrass prairie, where bison still roam free.

PRICES: Membership asks for a minimum donation at a special introductory price of $15. Ask about the special programs for children, *Adopt-an-Acre* ($35), *Adopt-a-Bison* ($25) and *Rescue-the-Reef* ($35). Many of the preserves and their programs are free to members. Some trips are used as fund-raisers and charge fairly hefty prices.

PRIMARILY FOR: Everyone "in reasonable health" is welcome to participate. Many descriptions detail the difficulty of trips that should help you determine if a particular trip is appropriate for your family.

BOOKED FOR TRAVEL

No matter where you roam in the U.S., Patricia Gordon and Reed C. Snow's **Kids Learn America,** *Bringing Geography to Life with People, Places & History,* makes use of creative learning techniques; children become familiar with our 50 states without the tedium of memorizing dry facts. The book is most appropriate for those who can read fluently. Everyone in the family will enjoy discovering new information. (Williamson)

SIERRA CLUB
Outing Department
85 Second Street
San Francisco, CA 94105
Phone: 415-977-5630
Fax: 415-977-5794

PROFILE: Founded in 1892 by a pioneer of the American conservation movement, John Muir, the club's initial goal was to protect the land of the Sierra Nevada. Today, the club's Outing Department sponsors more than two dozen trips exclusively for families. These trips aim to create an atmosphere that "allows children to experience the fun of outdoor living with other children. Everyone shares camp chores, outdoor skills and knowledge about area plants, animals and ecology." All trips are accompanied by a naturalist and welcome participants of diverse abilities and interests. The brochure is now more than 100 pages, with a separate section devoted to the family trips. A membership in Sierra Club is necessary in order to participate. Be certain to inquire about the activities of chapters in your area as they are likely to organize appealing family-friendly excursions.

PROGRAMS: Among the family-designated offerings: *Spring Canoe/Camp* trip in the Okefenokee Wildlife Refuge (children ages 6 and older); *Toddler Tromp* in Virginia's Prince William Forest Park (children 2 and older); *Gem of the Grand Canyon* (children ages 8 and older); *Kauai Family Adventure* (all ages); *A Week in the Teton Wilderness* (all ages); *Just for Grandparents and Grandchildren, Tahoe Forest in California* (children 5 and older); *Molokai and Maui Family Adventure* (children 8 and older); *Nature: A Capital View in Washington D.C.* (all ages).

A perennial favorite is the *Toddler Tromp in Acadia National Park* in Maine that introduces families to camping without the responsibility of cooking, planning and the like. Both the demands and needs of smaller children (generally young guests are from 2 to 14) and experienced, intrepid older kids and adults are taken into consideration. During the week you'll explore the Northeast's only national park with its rugged seashore, mountains and spectacular lakes, interconnected by hiking trails and roads. Van travel, hiking, a whale watch, a visit to the Sceanarium, a hike to Jordan Pond and tidepool explorations are all part of the experience.

PRICES: Memberships are $35/individual, $43/joint. The six-night/seven-day *Acadia Toddler Tromp* costs $640/adult, $425/child under 17; *Just For Grandparents*, five-night/six-day is $390/adult, $260/child.

PRIMARILY FOR: All ages will find excursions of interest.

BOOKED FOR TRAVEL

Any parent seeking expert guidance before heading into the wilderness with kids need look no further than **The Sierra Club Family Outdoors Guide:** *Hiking, Backpacking, Camping, Bicycling, Water Sports, and Winter Activities With Children* by Marlyn Doan. The book is filled with all-around practical advice on how to plan and what to expect, while acknowledging that outdoor adventures with babies and toddlers present special challenges. Doan never at a loss to suggest intelligent strategies to keep little ones safe and happy, and offers suggestions on how to motivate children to walk when they say they're tired, how to get them to accept carrying a backpack as a matter of course, what you must plan on if you travel with a child in diapers, and so much more. Much of the book is devoted to describing essential gear and a long list of suppliers is included. Finally, so you don't forget something crucial, a handy checklist of basic equipment is provided at the end of the book. (Sierra Club)

Muir of the Mountains is the biography of John Muir, the great pioneer of the American conservation movement and founder of the Sierra Club. Written for children in a very accessible style by U.S. Supreme Court Justice William O. Douglas, himself an ardent naturalist, it was first published in 1961 and has now been reissued in a slightly abridged form. Born in Scotland, Muir emigrated to this country with his family at age 11. He traveled widely throughout his life: at one point he walked 1,000 miles from Kentucky to the Gulf of Mexico. His story will not fail to speak to and inspire the nature lover in a child. (Little Brown)

UNDERWATER EXPLORERS SOCIETY (UNEXSO)

P.O. Box F42433
Freeport, Grand Bahama Island
The Bahamas
Phone: 809-373-1244
Fax: 809-373-8956

U.S. Address
P.O. Box 22878
Ft. Lauderdale, FL 33335
800-992-DIVE/305-351-9889
305-351-9740

PROFILE: Established in 1965, UNEXSO is one of the most respected dive organizations in the world and is an innovator of scuba diving expeditions such as open ocean dolphin dives and the shark dive. It is founder of *The Dolphin Experience* at Sanctuary Bay in the Bahamas, the largest dolphin research facility in the world. UNEXSO is "strongly committed to presenting our animals in a way that forces compassion for the survival of not only dolphins, but for all their aquatic relatives."

PROGRAMS: All options are offered with flexible schedules based on the needs of the dolphins, rather than those of the customer.

Certified scuba divers are encouraged to feed friendly bottlenose dolphins right from their hands during the *Dolphin Dive.* A *Dolphin Close Encounter* invites non-divers to observe these intelligent, friendly animals up close in a small, shallow enclosure at their site on Sanctuary Bay, home to 13 Atlantic bottlenose dolphins ranging in age from 2 months to 20 years. Though not a swim-with-the-dolphins experience, it is definitely a hands-on event, as personally witnessed by our own kids. What was most interesting to us during our visit was that while the dolphins are not in captivity and are free to leave at will, they opt to return daily. Another program of interest to certified divers is *Marine Identification*, taught by resident naturalist Ben Rose. This includes five hours of workshops with lectures and visual presentations followed by three dives (extra cost).

Children 16 and older may want to consider signing up for a full day as a *Dolphin Assistant Trainer*. Participants, in conjunction with the staff, are actively involved with the animal care in a variety of ways, from assisting in an open training session to setting up the food preparation area.

UNEXSO's brochures also include several lodging opportunities that feature children's programs if you decide not to bring your children to UNEXSO, or if they are too young for the experience you select. Among these choices are Club Fortuna Beach, Bahamas Princess Resort & Casino (where we happily stayed for four days) and the Lucayan Beach Resort and Casino. You need not purchase a lodging package to participate in UNEXSO's courses.

PRICES: The *Dolphin Dive* carries a $70 surcharge on normal dive packages. A one-tank dive is $35, $89 for three dives. The two-hour *Close Encounter* experience is $29/person; *Marine Identification* is

$99. *Dolphin Assistant Trainer* is $159 the first day with two- to five-day extensions offered for an additional charge.

PRIMARILY FOR: We saw children as young as 3 or 4 gleefully participate in the *Close Encounter* program. Generally, however, UNEXSO's guidelines call for children 5 and older.

WILDERNESS SOUTHEAST
711 Sandtown Road
Savannah, GA 31410-1019
Phone: 912-897-5108
Fax: 912-897-5116

PROFILE: This non-profit educational organization founded in 1973 plans its programs for participants who find nature "not an adversary to conquer, but a storehouse of infinite knowledge" and for travelers who recognize "that preserving the natural environment is essential to our future well-being." Friends who took a Wilderness Southeast trip were very impressed with the knowledge of the guides and how well they interacted and communicated with kids. On the other hand, they were totally unprepared for the vast number of mosquitoes present. Be sure to ask about this and bear in mind that the dates of your trip may be a determining factor.

PROGRAMS: The *Okefenokee Cabin/Canoe* (minimum age 8) trip is ideal for those who don't wish to camp, as travelers lodge in cozy cabins complete with showers. Days are spent exploring in a canoe, paddling different trails each day to observe alligators, wading birds and lily pads and to investigate the ecology of the swamp. *Sea Turtle Watch* (minimum age 12) is another lodge-based experience.

If camping is not too rugged for you, we recommend the *Cumberland Island Basecamp/Hike* (minimum age 8), where you explore this barrier island, designated as a National Seashore, from a forest basecamp adjacent to the beach. There's a bathhouse and cold showers.

For those who want to head for the Great Smokies, a *Basecamp/ Hike* trip is specifically designed for children as young as 5. During your visit you'll hike trails in the Little Cataloochee Valley, viewing wildflowers, streams, deer, birds, etc. On this family trip, the nature activities have been conceived with kids in mind.

A number of programs are offered exclusively for teenagers (sorry, no parents!).

PRICES: The four-day/three-night Okefenokee or Smokies trips are $450, 50 percent less for kids during the family departure; *Cumberland Island*, which operates in the spring, is $360. Children under 16 with one parent receive a 15 percent discount, with two parents a 25 percent discount.

PRIMARILY FOR: Each listing specifies age requirements: the youngest age taken is 5; several take children 8 and older; others are more appropriate with teenagers. Traditional, single-parent and multi-generational families are all welcome.

CHAPTER 3

TOUR OPERATORS & SPECIALIZED TRAVEL SERVICES

We're delighted to have found such a broad range of tour operators that truly enjoy having families along on their journeys. Several have been in the business of planning trips that welcome youngsters for many years; others are somewhat new at offering "family" tours, including a number of heavy hitters in the field of nature trips. Though one might believe their doing so is an attempt to capture a share of the family market, our understanding is slightly different. Actually, this group of operators (among them Abercrombie & Kent, Natural Habitat Adventures and Micato Safaris) have been accepting children for a long time and have recently realized that when families participate together, it's more fun for all concerned!

As veteran family travelers, we are continually surprised and pleased at the diverse ways in which trips have been reconfigured to meet unique family needs. Though many tour operators indicate age restrictions in their consumer material, rarely are these written in stone. Capability is the key factor, so always remember to use the ages stated as guidelines. For example, when the minimum age designated is 8 for a canoe trip and your 6-year-old has been canoeing and camping since age 3, a call to the tour operator detailing your child's experience may quickly make you eligible for a trip. Conversely, an intermediate rafting trip with a minimum age 10 may be too rigorous for your novice 12-year-old. Evaluate the maturity and flexibility of your kids. See page 12 for questions to ask before you book.

If being a "green" traveler is one of your personal goals, keep in mind that the truly environmentally-committed operators put their money where their mouths are and add to the economic well-being of the destination by utilizing lodging in locally owned hotels, hiring local guides at a fair wage, frequenting local restaurants and the like. An integral feature of all of these types of vacations is respect for the local people and their customs as well as for the environment.

ABERCROMBIE & KENT (A&K)
1520 Kensington Road
Oak Brook, IL 60521-2141
Phone: 800-323-7308/708-954-2944
Fax: 708-954-3324

PROFILE: A&K, which began as an African safari tour operator in 1962, has long been ranked in the top echelon of luxury adventure travel thanks to its ability to provide the best available travel package at any point on the globe it chooses to explore. Last year, A&K introduced a series of *Family Holidays*, which pay special attention to children, their interests and learning patterns. Best yet is their attitude: "Parents never need to worry if children will be welcome, or catered for, at any stop along the way — we've already taken care of all the logistical details involved. We're also careful to strike a good balance between time together (to explore in each other's company) — and time apart (to pursue separate activities as age and interest dictate.)" Unlike other tour operators who may cancel a trip due to a lack of paid bookings, A&K guarantees that tours found in their brochure will operate. Upon receipt of your deposit, you'll begin to receive reams of material, plus gobs of goodies, starting with *Preliminary Tour Information*, a flight bag, travel wallet and baggage tags. They even send a trip diary for your kids.

PROGRAMS: All A&K trips, which are limited to a maximum of 24 passengers, sound just terrific; we especially like the special activities planned for the kids. Its most unique journey, we believe, is *Antarctica, the Falklands and South Georgia Islands*, which sails out of Santiago aboard the expeditionary vessel *Explorer* and lasts 19 days in all. At every stop along the way you'll see wildlife — penguins, albatross and all varieties of seal. Four days are spent in Antarctica, penetrating its icy terrain by Zodiac. This Antarctic exploration takes place during the Antarctic summer, over the Christmas/New Year's school holiday.

On the 15-day *Kenya Family Safari*, which offers six annual departures, all ages are welcomed (nannies can be provided for little ones). In addition to visiting the incredible wildlife habitats of Amboseli National Park, Samburu National Reserve, Aberdare National Park and Maasai Mara National Reserve, stops include an animal orphanage, a village primary school, an ostrich farm and more.

On *A Family Holiday in Egypt*, which includes a cruise on the *Sun Boat* II (minimum age 10), there's an Egyptian treasure hunt and family activities on board in the evenings. Yet another incredible nature encounter can be had on the 11-day *Highlights of the Galapagos and Ecuador*.

New this year is a *Family Tour of Costa Rica,* which will be hosted by both a children's activity co-ordinator and a naturalist. There will be bird-watching lessons, game-spotting by boat in Tortuguero National Park (home to the major nesting area of the Atlantic Green Turtle), and a nature walk in the Cloud Forest Reserve followed by a visit to a local school to meet Costa Rican youngsters.

Other family trips head to Alaska, Britain, Australia, France, the Amazon and a dude ranch in Montana.

BOOKED FOR TRAVEL

In **Let's Go Traveling**, by Robin Rector Krupp, young readers can join Rachel Rose step-by-step along the way as she visits the wonders of the ancient world in this book which is part travelogue and part history lesson. Its highly pictorial and chatty format is sure to awaken the travel bug in any child at least 7 years of age. A great book! (Morrow)

PRICES: There are prices for adults, children under 12 and teens 13 to 18. There is a modest single supplement. Land rates for the *Family Tour of Costa Rica* are $2,170/adult, $1,750/child 12 or under, with a single supplement of $290. *Antarctica* tour prices which include air from Miami start at $7,995/adult, children 7 to 18/50 percent.

PRIMARILY FOR: Age restrictions vary, though many trips carry none. Multigenerational groups are included in most departures and single parents report feeling very comfortable on the trips.

ALASKA WILDLAND ADVENTURES (AWA)
P.O. Box 389
Girdwood, AK 99587
Phone: 800-334-8730/907-783-2928
Fax: 907-783-2130

PROFILE: Now in its 20th year, AWA was a pioneer in offering "environmentally sensitive natural history tours, backcountry lodging, and wilderness voyages." Run by Alaskans, AWA practices what it preaches by donating 10 percent of its earnings each year to a variety of environmentally aware groups. It's no wonder they have often been called Alaska's best Eco Tour operator.

PROGRAMS: Youngsters over 12 are welcome on the majority of AWA's trips, which go anywhere from the Kenai Peninsula and Denali National Park to Prince William Sound and the Arctic National Wildlife Refuge. However, each summer AWA offers the *Alaska Family Safari* which welcomes kids 6 to 11, that always fills up quickly. Perhaps such great demand will lead AWA to add extra sections in the future!

This trip begins in Anchorage and heads for Chugach State Park and National Forest for an overnight stay at a lodge alongside a scenic river. Among the highlights are a float trip where spawning salmon, eagles and moose are apt to be seen; a gentle hike through fields of wildflowers; a yacht tour of Kenai Fjords; a visit to the towns of Seward and Talkeetna and, of course, Denali National Park. Your cameras will capture the sea otters, puffins, seals, moose, sheep, caribou and grizzlies you're apt to pass. Alas, after a trip on the Alaska Railroad back to Anchorage, the trip comes to an end, but happily, add-ons can be customized for your family.

AWA also highly recommends its *Alaska Camping Adventure* for families with teens. This 10-day outing visits spots rarely seen by most tourists, while offering civilized amenities like hot showers, restaurant meals and several nights in B&Bs or lodges. Seven departure dates are offered.

PRICES: The *Family Safari* is $2,295/adult, double occupancy and $2,095/child under 12. Discounts are offered when children room with parents. The *Camping Adventure* ranges from $1,995 to $2,095 based on the accommodations you select. An early June departure offers a $200 discount.

PRIMARILY FOR: The *Family Safari* is specifically for families with children 6 to 11 and often has multigenerational groups as well as older siblings. For the *Camping* trip, children need to be at least 12 years old; some of the activities may be too rigorous for seniors.

AMERICAN WILDERNESS EXPERIENCE (AWE)
P.O. Box 1486
Boulder, CO 80306
Phone: 800-444-0099/303-444-2622
Fax: 303-444-3999

PROFILE: AWE is an unusual type of travel company, neither tour operator nor wholesaler. Rather, it acts as a clearing house for a number of both of these, working directly with consumers or with travel agents. Each season, AWE publishes brochures describing a wide variety of adventures, together with the names of the tour operators who run them. We encourage you, however, not to bypass AWE and go directly to the outfitter/tour operator. Contrary to what you might think, you're unlikely to realize any savings by doing so. Also, the particular trip that initially piqued your interest may turn out not to be your cup of tea. The folks at AWE will have lots of alternatives at their fingertips!

PROGRAMS: We asked AWE Director Dave Wiggins to highlight those trips which were most ideally suited to families. Much to our surprise and delight, more than half of the offerings in the brochure were highlighted with bright yellow marker. Among them was a three- or six-day horsepack trip to *Arizona's Superstition Wilderness* which includes riding next to towering saguaro cacti, exploring deep rock canyons and reveling in the beauty of the blooming Sonoran Desert. We were also turned on by the *Whale Watching/Camping* trip in Baja, California, which a friend of ours took with her then 6-year-old daughter and simply adored. Then there are the *Dolphin Discovery Camp* in Honduras (see page 172), a *Flathead River Ride & Raft* excursion and a *Pecos Wilderness Llama Trek*. The biggest problem is which one to select. We're tempted by the *Backside of Hawaii: Three Island Adventure*, which features hiking and snorkeling far from the tourist centers.

BOOKED FOR TRAVEL

For children ages 8 to 12, Chronicle's **Junior Nature Series** are young people's guides to regional American wildlife, both common and rare. Each book includes a map of area wildlife preserves. Having seen **Wildlife Southwest** and **Wildlife California**, we recommend taking them along when visiting either region. Additional titles include **Wildlife Pacific Northwest** and **Wildlife Alaska**. (Chronicle)

PRICES: Superstition Wilderness: Three-day: $450, six-day: $855, no youth discount. *Baja Whalewatch:* $1,495, no youth discount. *Dolphin Discovery:* $600-$825/adult, $500/child 8 to 14. *Flathead River Ride & Raft:* Four days, $560/adult, $500/child 8 to 12. *Pecos Wilderness Llama Trekking:* Five days, $695/adult, $665/ages 10 to 16 and seniors; *Backside of Hawaii:* $1,555, no youth discount.

PRIMARILY FOR: Superstition Wilderness, minimum age 7; *Baja Whalewatch,* minimum age 12; *Dolphin Discovery,* minimum age 8; *Flathead River Ride & Raft,* minimum age 8; *Pecos Wilderness Llama Trekking,* minimum age 10. *Backside of Hawaii,* minimum age 6. Though none of the above trips carry single supplements, those that do are noted in AWE's brochure. Grandparents who are "active, in good physical condition and health" are welcome. No experience is necessary with the exception of those scuba trips for certified divers.

ARCTIC TREKS
Box 73452
Fairbanks, AK 99707
Phone: 907-455-6502
Fax: 907-455-6522

PROFILE: Arctic Treks was organized in 1979 by experienced mountain guides Carol Kasza and Jim Campbell, who eventually married and became the parents of Kendra, now 14, and Kyle, 10. Arctic Treks is "committed to and active in the effort to protect the wilderness and promote ecotourism and minimum impact camping in Alaska's Brooks Range." Having spoken with them many times over the past dozen years, we were not surprised to learn that Carol is a past president of the *Alaska Wilderness Guides Association* and current vice-president of the *Alaska Wilderness Recreation & Tourism Association* and that Jim has designed and led trips for The Nature Conservancy, National Geographic and the BBC.

Jim and Carol have long welcomed families to explore their very special corner of the earth and have a good understanding for how youngsters fare in this wilderness. Both Kendra and Kyle have tested the trips Arctic Trek offers, with the exception of the harder backpack trips. Jim tells us that Kyle's currently lobbying to join one of these, but Jim wants to wait until Kyle is at least bigger than the pack he'll have to carry!

Don't be concerned about socialization for your kids when you join an Arctic Trek; on the customized family trips, Kyle and Kendra almost always join Carol and/or Jim.

PROGRAMS: Most suitable for families are the *High Arctic Basecamp* and *Day Hiking Trips*, both of which take place in isolated locations (accessible only by floatplane) selected for their remarkable beauty and abundant wildlife. The daily hiking ranges from leisurely strolls to challenging ridge hikes.

Parents with older children should consider a rafting trip. *Hulahula River Rafting* and *Konagkut River Rafting* pass through some class III rapids while *Canning River Rafting* is a somewhat gentler experience. On all three you'll enjoy day hikes to the haunts of bears, wolves, caribou, moose, falcons, hawks, eagles and more.

More than half of the trips operated each season are customized. All of the trips take place in the environs of Gates of the Arctic National Park and the Arctic National Wildlife Refuge.

PRICES: Prices are in the range of $200 to $250/adult, per day. There is a 10 percent discount for families.

PRIMARILY FOR: We know that Carol and Jim have taken children as young as 4. However, because of the remote wilderness environment, we highly recommend speaking with them directly.

BOOKED FOR TRAVEL

Let's Go To The Arctic: *A Story and Activities About Arctic People and Animals*, by Charlotte Ford Mateer with illustrations by Linda Witt Fries, recalls the traditional life of the Inuit (Eskimo) people as it was until recent years. You'll meet the animals of the polar region, find out how an igloo is made (with instructions on how to construct your own out of modeling dough), and learn to carve an amulet out of soap. The subject matter is very well presented and the projects worth trying. (Rinehart)

BORN FREE SAFARIS & TOURS
12504 Riverside Drive
North Hollywood, CA 91607
Phone: 800-372-3274/818-981-7185
Fax: 818-981-8312

PROFILE: We first heard about Born Free from one of our contributors who wanted to go to Africa with her 11-year-old daughter to experience that continent's incredible wildlife, but was reluctant to go on an organized, traditional safari. Not only did Born Free offer her many options, she was also particularly impressed by the agent she worked with, who truly listened to her requirements — her lack of desire to move around too much or to bounce up and down in a vehicle every day, and so on. She picked a trip to South Africa, in part because the cost was under $200/day for the two of them during the safari portion of the trip. Their first stop was smack in the middle of the veldt, at the Palace Hotel, a safari-themed extravaganza in Sun City. Casinos, a fabulous waterpark, a crocodile farm and bush drives kept them busy for a few days before they headed for Honeyguide, a tented camp adjacent to what used to be the blacks-only section of Kruger National Park. Here game-viewing was obviously more important than other scheduled events (one night in the middle of dinner, a ruckus erupted in the bush and everyone gathered into jeeps to see what was going on, leaving food on the table). Then they visited the Zulu homelands, a completely different terrain in Maputaland and stayed at two lodges run by Conservation Corporation, one of the largest ecologically-minded outfits in the world. Phinda Forest Lodge, surrounded by beautiful palms, aloe trees and acacias, offered nearby beaches and the magnificent Umbalozi River for canoeing and birding. A half-hour away, in a completely different landscape was Nyala Lodge — great food, great company, great excursions. Before returning to civilization, they stopped at Harry's, a deluxe low-key lodge on the famous Mala-Mala Reserve. Their last evening was spent in total luxury at Sandton Towers near Johannesburg. It was quite a trip.

We spoke with Born Free President, Alana Hayden, who was very quick to point out that there are major differences between South African and East African safaris. In her educated opinion, the true African National Geographic experience is only found in East Africa, i.e., Kenya, Tanzania, etc. In South Africa the ambience tends to be more European. According to Hayden, who has taken both of her own kids to Africa on many occasions, family adventures in Africa are "the most enriching and educational weeks that you will ever spend together." When we asked her what Born Free's minimum age was, her answer was just the one we like to hear: "There's no real minimum age. It depends on the experiences of the child and the expectations of the parents. We've had children as young as 2. Oftentimes we can arrange for a private vehicle for a family with very young children who might not be able to keep up with a group or who feel that their children might have to alter their behavior when in the company of other adults." And, all of the trips in Born Free's impressive brochure can be customized for families.

PROGRAMS: Hakuna Matata is a 15-day family safari to Tanzania and Kenya, departing New York via Amsterdam (stopovers can be arranged). Accompanying guides have been chosen because they love kids and relate so well to them and to their interests. Guides give lessons in Swahili and are a fount of information about the many species of wildlife. It's hard to speak of highlights on such a trip since every day brings something new and extraordinary. Among the stops on the itinerary are the Ngorongoro Crater, called by some the "Cradle of Mankind," Mt. Kilimanjaro, Amboseli Game Reserve, the Giraffe Center (which offers an optional overnight stay at Giraffe Manor), the William Holden Orphanage and, of course, Massai-Mara. Born Free is great at organizing custom safaris. The unforgettable South African experience reported above is just one possibility.

PRICES: Hakuna Matata: $3,199 to $3,649/adult, $1,999 to $2,199/child under 12. Single supplement: $295 to $695.

PRIMARILY FOR: As stated above, there's no official minimum age. Brochure states that "all safari groups arranged according to the age range of the families traveling."

BOOKED FOR TRAVEL

Start with the *Animal Index* of **Africa's Top Wildlife Countries**, by Mark W. Nolting, to locate the habitat(s) of the animals you'd most like to encounter. Then read about what sort of travel is entailed to reach your goal and what to expect once you arrive. This book, though fascinating, is clearly aimed at the adult traveler; you'll need to consult additional sources if planning a family trip. (Global Travel)

FAMILY EXPLORATIONS, INC. (FEI)
343 Dartmouth Avenue
Swarthmore, PA 19081-1017
phone: 800-WE-GO-TOO/610-543-6200
Fax: 610-543-6262

PROFILE: Calling itself *The Nature and Cultural Tour Company for Families with Children*, FEI "heads to destinations of ecological and cultural significance in small groups with a loosely structured, informal atmosphere." Though a relative newcomer to the roster of exclusively family tour operators, Family Explorations appears to be well on the road to becoming a major player. Started in 1994 by Ken Klothen, an avid traveler who has done extensive travel with his own family, FEI espouses many of the values we so admire: "Foreign travel is never wasted on children. Our trips are planned so kids have time to settle in, feel at home and get into the rhythm of life in the host country. Accommodations have been specially chosen for their welcoming attitude toward families with children. We do everything possible to free you from everything except having a good time. Daily kids activities provide you time each day to spend with other adults or on your own plus every day you'll have time together with your kids and time to spend as you choose." Each trip features age-appropriate activities just for kids and welcomes any age child to participate. We especially like the fact that they encourage bookings from travel agents. Prior to your trip, your kids will be sent postcards from the counselors who will be accompanying them. A second letter is sent to you, detailing everything from necessary documents and money matters to currency and packing recommendations, together with a short biography of the tour leaders.

PROGRAMS: From rather simple beginnings — a trip to Costa Rica where Ken Klothen had visited extensively (to the point of buying property there) — the company now also runs trips to Belize, Brazil, Ecuador, Canada, Ireland, Italy, South Africa and the U.S. All of the four- to 15-day itineraries are bound to fascinate you.

The most nature-oriented trips which include good wildlife viewing possibilities visit *Belize*, where the group visits a baboon sanctuary, canoes down a tropical river and snorkels in crystal clear waters; *Costa Rica,* with visits to a tropical rain forest, a dry tropical forest and a cloud forest, a walk through a mangrove and a float down a river; *South Africa/Swaziland* and its incredible game parks — Kalahari Gemsbok National Park, Kruger National Park and the Mlilwane Game Reserve in Swaziland — which are natural habitats for lion, leopard, elephant, buffalo, rhinoceros, baboon, kudu, hippo and more. It's a dazzling itinerary, quite different from most other family trips to Africa, which tend to confine themselves to East Africa.

PRICES: *Belize* is priced at $1,850/adult, $1,350/child under 12; *Costa Rica* is $1,400/adult, $1,000/child under 12. On some trips children's prices are valid for youngsters up to 14 or 15. Occasionally, there are special prices for teenagers.

PRIMARILY FOR: All family configurations and children of all ages are welcomed.

GRANDTRAVEL
c/o The Ticket Counter, Inc.
6900 Wisconsin Avenue
Suite 706
Chevy Chase, MD 20815
Phone: 800-247-7651/301-986-0790
Fax: 301-913-0166

PROFILE: 1996 celebrates the 10th anniversary of this unique travel company founded by grandmother Helena Koenig, whose goal is still to: "Support grandparents in their efforts to foster, nurture and actively participate in the cultural enrichment of their grandchildren's lives." From a total of four departures in year one, Grandtravel now offers more than 35 departures on a total of 17 travel opportunities. Not all of the trips take in our natural environment, some head to cities and resorts. All of the tours are teacher-escorted (in addition to providing the services of an on-site guide) and schedule lots of time together combined with separate activities for the different age groups. Most intelligently, two departure dates are planned for each itinerary, one for children 7 to 11, the other for those 12 to 17. There are even a few trips with mixed ages for families where there are grandchildren in both the younger and older groupings.

Koenig's attention to detail, her keen understanding of the needs and desires of both age groups and her appreciation of the special shared intergenerational relationship combine to ensure that these trips will never be forgotten.

PROGRAMS: One of the trips which is particularly nature-oriented heads for the *Pacific Northwest*, visiting Seattle, the San Juan Islands, Mt. Rainier, Blake Island and Victoria. Both en route to the San Juan Islands and during a deep sea salmon fishing trip in Victoria, you'll have the opportunity to observe porpoises, bald eagles, orca and minke whales and sea otters. Mt. Rainier National Park is a world of craggy peaks, waterfalls and canyons, which can be experienced up close on a breathtaking nature walk or afar through a telescope. Blake Island has forests and beaches; it is the ancestral fishing grounds of the Suquamish Indians, whose cultural tradition of longhouses and totem poles draws visitors throughout the year.

An awesome journey, *Alaskan Wilderness Adventure*, features a Mendenhall Glacier Float trip, goldpanning in Gold Creek, a visit to a musk ox farm and sensational wildlife viewing in Denali Park.

There are many other North American destinations, including one that visits the Grand Canyon. Folks looking for a combination of foreign culture mixed with the great outdoors should check out *Barging on the Waterways of Holland and Belgium; Switzerland: A Place of Neutrality; Kenya Adventure Safari*; or *Australia Down Under/Outback*.

PRICES: These trips are not cheap yet they offer good value considering all that is included, beginning with two group leaders and gobs of pre-planning assistance. *Pacific Northwest:* $3,490/person/double, $3,285/person/triple — land only. *Alaskan Wilderness:* $5,990/adult/double, $5,780/adult/triple, $5,530/child/double, $5,310/child/triple — land only.

PRIMARILY FOR: Minimum age is 7. Prices are designed not to penalize a single grandparent. In addition, the company plans individual trips which might include all three generations celebrating a special occasion or just wishing to get together in a unique environment.

52 Nature Activities, a recent addition to Chronicle Books' decks of travel cards, is a real winner. Lynn Gordon is the clever idea-lady here and Susan Synarski has added the visual appeal. The majority of the suggestions can be tried alone but, for some a partner can be enlisted. The cards are equally usable at home or away (there's nothing easier than packing a deck of cards). We like the way they encourage a child to look closely at things, both inside his or her own mind and feelings and outside at the world at large. (Chronicle)

JOURNEYS
4011 Jackson Road
Ann Arbor, MI 48103
Phone: 800-255-8735/313-665-4407
Fax: 313-665-2945

PROFILE: Will and Joan Weber met in college and went on to Nepal where he was a Peace Corps volunteer and she taught at the International School. They founded Journeys in 1978, while they were graduate students back in the United States, because of their desire to share their ideals of travel and cultural exchange with friends. At the same time, they established the non-profit *Earth Preservation Fund* (EPF) — "through which travelers can assist and encourage better conservation and environmental practices at a local level worldwide." The Webers were pioneers in forging tourism partnerships with local guides and are considered leaders in their field. Nearly 20 years since Journeys' inception, its roster of offerings is awesome.

About eight years ago, Journeys began offering just-for-family departures to several destinations. The Webers and their children, now ages 8 and 14, often accompany these journeys. The pre-departure material (itineraries, foreign phrase booklet, etc.) sent to participants, comes attractively ensconced in a vinyl, velcroed, zippered fold-up pack along with the participant roster, final reminder notice, T-shirt, luggage tags, visa application form, a trip diary for each child, and a 28-page booklet with biographies of the Webers, plus details on health precautions, jet lag strategies, security, and recommendations on "making a good impression as a Traveler." There's even a flier entitled *A Code of Ethics for Nature and Culture Travelers* from the EPF. We have never had the opportunity to join one of Journeys' expeditions but have received numerous glowing reports. One in particular stressed the quality of the on-site guides, who took such good care of their group— which seemed not to be the case with other groups they met up with. Our many conversations over the past eight years with both Will and Joan continue to reconfirm our enthusiasm for their endeavors.

PROGRAMS: For the family programs, small groups of four to six families travel together. Trips are scheduled to coincide with school vacations and most of them can be customized at comparable prices.

WAWA (Week After Week Adventures) are usually week-long excursions, specifically designed for those with time limitations, and often attract families. All of the trips are graded according to difficulty and many are open to families. *WAWAs* visit Tanzania, Kenya, Nepal, Belize, Panama, Costa Rica, Bolivia, Peru, the Galapagos Islands and Thailand.

Among the just-for-family choices:

15-day *Million Animal Family Safari*, a wildlife/cultural excursion that brings participants into contact with Maasai and Kenyan children, departs in July/August. Also in August, the 13-day *Australia Family Odyssey* visits a rain forest, cruises the Great Barrier Reef and heads for the outback.

There are three excursions scheduled over the Christmas holiday break season: During the 16-day *Annapurna Family Trek*, children under 60 pounds ride in Sherpa-carried baskets; the 8-day *Family Rain Forest Discovery in Costa Rica* travels deep into jungle along the Pacific coast for some of the best tropical bird and animal viewing in the world; and the week-long *Panama Family Discovery* is the only family trip we know of to this land, which most people only associate with its famous canal, though it contains many natural treasures as well. On the itinerary are Barro Colorado Nature Monument, a tropical rain forest which has been protected since 1923; the San Blas Islands where you'll meet the native Kuna Indians, travel by dugout canoe and snorkel; and Amistad International Park, home to many quetzal and bell birds; and the Panama Canal.

Over spring break, a *Belize Family Explorer* tracks wild animals, snorkels the world's second largest barrier reef and learns the myths and mysteries of the Mayans.

If you're undecided on which trip most appeals to you, ask for a copy of the trip review notes which are written by Will and/or Joan when they return from a family journey and report both their impressions and those of the kids on the trip.

PRICES: All are land-only: *Million Animal Safari*: $2,345/adult, $1,995/child. *Australia Family Odyssey*: $2,595/adult, $995/child. *Annapurna Family Trek*: $1,345/adult, $890/child. *Family Rain Forest Discovery* (Costa Rica): $1,290/adult, $890/child. *Panama Family Explorer*: $1,250/adult, $850/child. *Belize Family Explorer*: $1,350/adult, $890/child. Youngsters ages 12 and under sharing with two adults are considered children. Teens who share with two adults may also receive discounted prices.

BOOKED FOR TRAVEL

When Hippo Was Hairy And Other Tales From Africa, as told by Nick Greaves, is a delightful collection of 36 traditional animal stories from folklore, accompanied by facts about the habits and habitats of these same animals. (Barron's)

PRIMARILY FOR: On the family departures, 5 is the suggested minimum age. Participants are typically ages 8 to 15. The customized trips take youngsters from age 3. All standard departures with difficulty designations of I or II welcome families with children 10 and older. Because of their years of experience, Journeys has a pretty good idea of which trips other families will be booking. Grandparents are very welcome and multigenerational groups are quite common.

MICATO SAFARIS
15 West 26th Street
New York, NY 10010
Phone: 800-642-2861/212-545-7111
Fax: 212-545-8297

PROFILE: Micato Safaris is owned and operated by the Pinto family, whose members have been born and raised in Kenya since the turn of the century. Those involved in Micato Safaris are natives in the land they endeavor to share with your family. Because of this heritage, Micato opens doors that are closed to other safari operators, including a farewell dinner in Nairobi at their family home.

There are quite a number of designated-for-family departures from which to choose. The company headquarters are in Nairobi, but a Pinto (Dennis) sits firmly at the helm of the North American office as well. Micato guarantees every departure date in its catalog, regardless of the number of participants. Close friends of ours traveled with Micato (before they added special family departures) and were most gratified when Micato was able to arrange a special visit just for them to meet the child they had adopted through the Save the Children Fund. What a wonderful day!

PROGRAMS: *The Family Safari* begins its 14-day journey with two nights in Nairobi, visiting The Giraffe Centre and the Langata Ostrich Farm at feeding time. Then you're whisked off to Ol Pejeta Ranch and Rhino Reserve, a short distance from the new Chimpanzee Sanctuary built by the Jane Goodall Institute, where you'll stay in luxury tents, complete with bathrooms, at Sweetwaters Tented Camp. Over the next few days you'll travel into the Northern Frontier through the Shaba

Game Reserve, to Lake Baringo and the Great Rift Valley, stopping to visit the local village before heading for Lake Nakuru, where there's a unique opportunity to visit a local school. After two-and-a-half awesome days in the Maasai Mara, it's back to Nairobi and a farewell to Africa. Kids, who receive a goodie bag prior to departure, can expect to learn a Swahili song and be served milk and cookies at tea time in addition to the several special stops mentioned above.

PRICES: Land prices start at $3,295/adult, $2,995/teens 13 to 18 and $2,265/child, depending upon date of departure. Single supplements are $755/adult, $655/teenager. Micato has a no tipping policy.

PRIMARILY FOR: This trip is designed for parents and/or grandparents. Age 2 is the "absolute age restriction for children." The recommended age is about 7.

NATURAL HABITAT ADVENTURES (NHA)
2945 Center Green Court South
Boulder, CO 80301
Phone: 800-543-8917/303-449-3711
Fax: 303-449-3712

PROFILE: NHA, now in its 11th year, is one of our country's most highly respected nature tour operators, presenting an exciting array of nature vacations across the globe. "What makes our tours unique is that we concentrate on the animals of a given region, rather than on the region itself," says founder Ben Bressler. Consequently, though departures are offered year-round, each destination is seasonal, taking into account animal migrations, breeding seasons and the best weather conditions for animal viewing. Though NHA has long welcomed children on its trips, as we've witnessed ourselves, this is the first year that there are actually specific tours and dates designated as *Family Programs*.

PROGRAMS: One of the most exhilarating trips we've taken was NHA's *Seal Watch*, a trip which took us to the vast floating ice floes of Eastern

Canada where each March, 250,000 harp seals bear their young. The trip begins in Halifax, where the small group boards a flight for the Magdalene Islands in the Gulf of St. Lawrence. Over the next three days, weather permitting, guests don expedition suits and board helicopters in search of seal herds, observing their rapid development on a daily basis. While the mother seals are off feeding, the fluffy white pups (which are everywhere) may be approached; quite a few of them are amenable to petting. When you can't visit the ice, there's plenty of activity back in and around the hotel — nature hikes, ice-skating, snowshoeing, cross-country skiing, night tubing and more. The staff was terrific — young, energetic and sociable on the one hand, very responsible and knowledgeable about the seals and how to handle the frozen terrain on the other. We always had fun and we always felt safe. Also, the kids fit easily into the program and didn't experience a minute of boredom.

Family Kenya & Tanzania, a 12-day safari focusing on education and family interaction, is one of NHA's first family trips. While visiting the homeland of elephant, rhinoceros, buffalo, leopard, cheetah, lion, wildebeest, hippopotamus, zebra, gazelle, giraffe, impala, waterbuck, birdlife, warthogs and more, you'll stay in unique mobile tented camps that provide "all of the comforts of the very best lodges but give us the added advantage of the untouched seclusion found in the outback." Areas explored include Maasai Mara, Lake Manyara, the Serengeti, Olduvai Gorge and Ngorongoro Crater.

Other designed-for-family trips are *Family Alaska* and *Family Costa Rica*. Still to come from NHA are *Churchill (Canada) Summer*, the *Galapagos Islands* and, perhaps, their renowned *Dolphin Watch*.

PRICES: Seal Watch prices are based on how often you choose to go out to the ice floes, and range from $1,695-$2,695/person. There is a single supplement of $285. *Family Kenya & Tanzania* is $3,595/adult, $2,195/child under 12, $795/single supplement.

PRIMARILY FOR: Seal Watch accepts very young children (they've taken children as young as 2). We, however, believe that it is best for children 6 and older. There is no official minimum age for the African trip, but if you contemplate traveling with a pre-schooler, you need to discuss it with NHA.

Guaranteed to delight animal lovers of any age, Richard and Jonah (age 8) Sobol's **Seal Journey** is a first-person story in photo-journalistic style that captures the world of the baby harp seals of the Gulf of St. Lawrence in their first few weeks of life. Husband and son of FTT contributor Ronnie Mae Weiss, they made the trip last winter, departing from Prince Edward Island. Richard Sobol is a noted photo- grapher of wildlife and if there were not one word of text his pictures would make a satisfying book all by themselves. However, we're glad he did decide to tell the story. It's not only interesting, it teaches an important ecological lesson. (Cobblehill)

NATURE EXPEDITIONS INTERNATIONAL (NEI)
474 Willamette Street
P.O. Box 11496
Eugene, OR 97440
Phone: 800-869-0639/541-484-6529
Fax: 541-484-6531

PROFILE: For the past 23 years, NEI has been operating trips which "allow everyone to be a modern explorer of planet Earth." Unfortunately, little in its consumer brochure indicates the enthusiasm towards families that NEI's Travel Agent Guidelines communicate: "Over the years, NEI has taken hundreds of families on special departures of our existing programs and has worked closely with them to ensure a safe and rewarding adventure for the entire family. We work directly with outfitters to alter and fine-tune the itineraries to accommodate the specific needs of any given family."

The more than 30 NEI programs visit South America, Central America, Africa, Asia, North America, and Oceania and there are cruises to Antarctica, Alaska and the Arctic and the South Pacific. The average group size is small (usually about a dozen participants), with departures guaranteed for as few as six.

Each trip is led by an expert in his/her field, all of whom hold masters degrees, Ph.D.s or the foreign equivalents, plus the assistance of local naturalist guides in each country.

PROGRAMS: In addition to being able to customize any of its tours for families, quite a few of its wildlife expeditions, including its new adventure cruises, are "ideal for families," according to NEI President Chris Kyle. Based on the itineraries Chris sent us, both the *Upper Amazon Adventure* and *The Great Land: Alaska Wildlife Expedition* operate during school vacation periods.

The *Upper Amazon Adventure* takes your family to explore the Upper Amazon River in Peru by plane, motorboat, dugout canoe and on foot. Staying at the Explorama Lodge, the Amazon Center for Environmental Education and Research and Explornapo Camp, you'll venture into the dense jungle where more than 1,800 species of bird, 2,000 varieties of fish and more than 200 land mammals reside. Highlights include walking along the "medicine trail," birding on a canopy walkway and visiting local river inhabitants. The eight-day trip offers an optional week-long extension to Cuzco, Machu Picchu and the Urubamba Valley in Peru.

Mammoth glaciers, enormous bears, and multitudes of salmon are among the sights to behold on the *Alaska Wildlife Expedition.* Departing from Seattle, nine- and 15-day trips begin with an overnight in Sitka followed by a flight to Glacier Bay for a day of hiking and a full-day of sailing various inlets on the catamaran *Spirit of Adventure.* Puffins, cormorants and black oystercatchers are in abundance on the rugged shores, while whales, porpoises and seals swim along tidewater glaciers. The next four days are devoted to exploring the Kenai Peninsula — hiking to Russian Falls, rafting the Kenai River, and boating through Cheval Narrows to Aialik Bay — all areas with unparalleled wildlife viewing. The optional second week concentrates on Denali National Park, that unspoiled wilderness home of grizzly bear, moose, caribou and golden eagles. Yet another three-day extension visits Katmai, a land with moonlike topography, best known for its volcanic history and many grizzlies.

The Pacific Northwest Adventure: On The Trail of Lewis & Clark follows in the path of these great explorers to that vastly diverse region in Oregon and Washington states known as Ecotopia — six distinct geographic zones in close proximity: rocky coast, mountain ranges, rainforest, grassland, chaparral and desert. The great appeal of this trip is that all this diversity is within our country's boundaries, something many may not realize.

PRICES: The *Upper Amazon Adventure* is $1,690/adult, with a $250 single supplement. The Cuzco/Machu Picchu extension is $1,090. *Alaska Wildlife* is $2,690/9 days, $3,790/15 days plus air from Seattle. The Katmai extension is $1,090. *On the Trail of Lewis & Clark* is $1,790/9 days, $2,690/16 days. Children 12 and under receive a 15 percent discount, teens 13 to 17, 10 percent.

PRIMARILY FOR: NEI recommends calling directly about minimum age guidelines, as they differ from trip to trip. In general, NEI prefers that children be 10 years of age and in good physical condition. The majority of trips would be suitable for multigenerational groups.

OFF THE BEATEN PATH (OTBP)
109 East Main Street
Bozeman, MT 59715
Phone: 800-445-2995/406-586-1311
Fax: 406-587-4147

PROFILE: We've known Pam and Bill Bryan since the early days of OTBP back in 1987. Their unique, highly individualized *Personal Itinerary Planning Service* delivers what it promises: "See and experience the Rocky Mountain West . . . the special people and places . . . more than the usual tourist itinerary . . . most rewarding experience involving the region's people, wildlife, land and space." OTBP travels from the northern peaks of the Canadian Rockies to the canyons of New

Mexico, and everywhere in-between — Montana, Wyoming, Idaho, Utah, Colorado and Arizona. Twenty national parks, countless canyons, acres of desert and spectacular mountains invite exploration.

No one can help you and your kids investigate this region better than OTBP. Whether you want to live in the lap of luxury or rough it in sleeping bags; have every step of your day planned or prefer to take things as they come with less structure; whether you're intrepid adventure types or vacation-only recreationers, OTBP works in close collaboration with you to design the trip of your dreams. Friends of ours took a trip with OTBP seven years ago, when their girls were 3 and 7, and they're still raving about it. They spent one day with a naturalist, another on an Indian Reservation, a few days at a ranch and much more.

PROGRAMS: There are no set itineraries other than what you plan for yourselves. We asked Pam to send us a sample program for a family of four and we received a 55-page printout for a trip planned last summer. This family started its trip in Idaho Falls, took a four-day river rafting trip on the Main Salmon River, headed into Lewis & Clark and Indian country before overnighting in Nevada City. Then it was off to Chico Hot Springs. After taking the waters, they drove to Cody, Wyoming, the Eastern gateway to Yellowstone National Park. The trip culminated in a few days of R&R at Spring Creek Ranch in Jackson (plus a recommended wildlife safari with Great Plains Wildlife Institute, see page 121). From the moment of arrival in Idaho Falls, OTBP provided specific driving instructions (even noting where construction was in progress) often with alternatives, interesting side trips, restaurant recommendations with options, shopping, cultural and recreational opportunity reports all along the way (looking for a Patagonia outlet or a hot air balloon trip?), not to mention securing tickets to an opera, a guided nature hike, an afternoon on horseback and, well, about 54 pages more!

It's unlikely that OTBP won't be able meet your expectations. They know, and understand, the difference between accommodating and welcoming children. Pam and Bill have taken their now teenaged children throughout their territory.

A first in '96 are OTBP's small group departures, one of which is specifically aimed at families: *Family Montana Ranch Adventure*, using a working ranch that does not accept individual bookings. Enjoy daily riding, guided hiking, a naturalist-guided trip into Yellowstone, a rafting trip, evening program, great fishing and children's activities. Offered twice over the summer, this is a unique ranching experience. Additional family trips are still in the planning stages.

PRICES: Personal Itinerary Planning costs $70/hour. A one-week trip averages between four and seven hours to complete, depending upon its complexity. OTBP gives more specific guidelines after speaking with you. The itinerary above cost $600. *Montana Family Ranch Adventure* is $2,240/adult, $1,935/child under 7.

PRIMARILY FOR: Absolutely anyone can be included in your trip. Trips can be paced to cater to the needs of even the very young. Multigenerational groups are quite common.

BOOKED FOR TRAVEL

Activity cum coloring books are a great way to get kids interested and involved in new places they visit. **Cecil's Montana Adventure**, by Sheri Amsel, teaches about animals and nature with mazes, word games, etc., and its relevance extends well beyond the boundaries of the Treasure State; take it along on any trip out west. (Falcon)

OH, TO BE IN ENGLAND ...
2 Charlton Street
New York, NY 10014
Phone: 212-255-8739
Fax: 212-986-8365

PROFILE: Owner Jennifer Dorn has been taking family trips to England since her son, now 21, was just three months old. Oh, To Be In England is a small personalized service where day-by-day itineraries are specifically designed for individual families. Jennie's personal knowledge will serve you well, whether this is your first or 50th trip to Britain. Jennie does not secure your reservations, though she supplies price guidelines, contacts and telephone/fax numbers to you or your travel agent. The one exception is at Tophams Ebury Court Hotel, a small, charming, moderately-priced property in London. If you book the Ebury Court, Jennie's services are on the house.

PROGRAMS: We asked Jennie for a sample, short, nature-oriented trip and she chose the Yorkshire Dales, an area not quite as well-known as say the Cotswolds or the Lake District, and one where she has success-fully sent several different configurations of families.

Using the town of Hawes as a base, at the center of the Yorkshire Dales National Park, you'll find yourselves in the heart of James Herriot country. Stay at Simonstone Hall, a 250-year-old mansion with 20th century comforts and luxuries and a warm welcome for children. Basic rates include breakfast; dinner is served as well. The first days' outings include a stop to sample locally made Wensleydale cheese and Bannock Cake, another regional favorite, before or after checking out the Upper Dales Folk Museum and Hardraw Force, the highest waterfall in England. Day two brings you to Wensleydale, which Jennie considers the "most beautiful of the Yorkshire Dales." Stop en route for lunch in Askrigg, once a world-famous clockmaking town, and carry on to Aysgarth Village and its not-to-be-missed Bolton Castle, an imposing structure dating back to the 14th century. Throughout the day you'll be lured into parking your car to take some of the many paths that lead over the dales in all directions. Save your last day for Swaledale, near Muker, where the hillsides are dotted with the distinctive local sheep whose wool is handknitted into all sorts of sweaters, scarves and hats by local villagers.

PRICES: Jennie's personalized itineraries cost from $175 to $250. The Ebury Court rates with full English breakfast are about $175/doubles with bath, $200/triples. Rates at the 10-room Simonstone Hall, includ-ing VAT and breakfast, are $155 to $210.

TRAVEL WITH YOUR CHILDREN

40 Fifth Avenue
New York, N.Y. 10011

(212) 477-5524
Fax: (212) 477-5173

PUBLISHERS OF:
FAMILY TRAVEL TIMES®
CRUISING WITH CHILDREN™

May 1996

Dear FTT Subscriber:

· Well, it's finally here — GREAT NATURE VACATIONS WITH YOUR KIDS — the first book in our Great Vacations With Your Kids series.

When we changed FTT to a quarterly in order to be able to have the time to write these guides, we kept track of how many issues you were entitled to as a result of this switch.

The label on the envelope this came in indicates how many issues you are owed. For each two issues we owe you, you are entitled to receive one book, the first one of which is enclosed. Subsequent books will be sent to you as they are published.

If the aforementioned number above is an odd number, we will issue you a credit towards the purchase of the next volume when we have fulfilled our commitment to you.

If you have any questions, or would like to convert your credit towards extending your subscription in lieu of receiving books, please put this request to us in writing and we will do our best to please you.

As always, here's to Great Vacations With Your Kids!

Dorothy Jordon

PRIMARILY FOR: Jennie offers suggestions for absolutely all ages and all possible family configurations. She chose the Yorkshire Dales because young children have lots of space to expend energy while older kids are also turned on by the available activities.

OVERSEAS ADVENTURE TRAVEL (OAT)
625 Mt. Auburn Street
Cambridge, MA 02138
Phone: 800-221-0814/617-876-0533
Fax: 617-876-0455

PROFILE: OAT has been in business for 18 years, offering "cultural and wildlife explorations that are conducted in small groups, with unique lodgings, unconventional modes of transportation, opportunities for varied levels of physical activity and expert trip leadership." Its former owner began offering family trips in 1988. Today, new owners are in the process of re-evaluating their family programs and have limited current family possibilities to two trips.

PROGRAMS: The *Serengeti Tented Safari* is a 17-day trip that features spectacular game viewing drives combined with an emphasis on cultural interaction. Participants will visit Maasai homes, a school and a marketplace. One departure date is scheduled for late June.

A *Family Costa Rica Nature Trip* takes place in March and December, during school vacation periods. The 10-day itinerary departs from Miami, visiting Costa Rica's national parks, rain forests, cloud forests and volcanoes. There's a local family-hosted dinner, rafting, kayak touring, horseback riding, a variety of hikes, swamp exploration and time to play on the beach.

PRICES: The *Serengeti Tented Safari* is $5,290/adult, $4,790/child ages 6 to 11 and includes air from New York or Boston. *Costa Rica*, including air from Miami, is $1,990/adult, $130/child less sharing.

PRIMARILY FOR: Children 6 and older are welcome to participate.

RASCALS IN PARADISE
650 Fifth Street
Suite 505
San Francisco, CA 94017
Phone: 800-U-RASCAL/415-978-9800
Fax: 415-442-0289

PROFILE: We first wrote about Rascals in early 1988, not long after they offered their first *Special Family Week.* Truly the "first kid on the block," offering travel packages designed specifically for families, founders Theresa Detchemendy and Deborah Baratta continue to use their own children as guinea pigs to field test each new trip. From their first trip to Namale Plantation in Fiji, Rascals' current destinations include: Fiji, Palau, Papua New Guinea, the Galapagos, Africa, Australia, New Zealand, Indonesia, Israel, the Caribbean, the Bahamas, Belize, Costa Rica, Honduras, Mexico and the United States, including a spectacular nature trip in Alaska.

Rascals says it is "about exploration, limitless horizons. Our vacations are classrooms without walls. Travel teaches us about traditions and tolerance; it teaches us about history and artistic creation; it nurtures aesthetic ambition. We learn to protect our oceans and forests and respect our neighbors as we experience the countless differences that enrich our world."

Rascals *Family Weeks* are unique. They put together small groups of three to six families with a teacher/escort who travels with the group to arrange fun activities for the accompanying children. Babysitters are included for parents of young children. Don't expect a full-time children's program. These trips are designed for parents and kids to spend time together but also for time for children and adults to do their own thing. *Family Weeks* operate in places that do not normally operate their own children's activities.

As they've grown, Rascals has added to its roster of trips. In addition to *Family Weeks* are *Kids Klub* resorts and *Family Friendly* resorts, some of which have been selected for their excellent scuba diving opportunities, others because they're just fabulous resorts.

PROGRAMS: With such a variety of trips, it's impossible to detail all of them here. Scuba divers might want to join the *Divers With Kids and Teens Family Weeks* in Honduras, Fiji, the Bahamas or their value-priced packages to Mexico's Akumal or Buenavista, where the wonders of the seas are brought to life. We're particularly turned on by the expedition to *Papua New Guinea*. From the emerald moss forest near the Great Tari Basin to the vast Sepik Plains and jungles of Karawari, this 15-day journey visits coffee plantations, village homesteads, floats down the Sepik River crossing into Irian Jaya and the Chambri Lakes, observing abundant wildlife while experiencing traditional tribal cultures.

Africa, The Real Zoo, departs several times a year and can be organized for individual families as well. After a day and night in Nairobi, your group heads north to Mweiga in the Aberdares and a luxurious game observation lodge, The Ark. Birds, bushbuck, elephant, buffalo, rhino, forest hog and even the rare and elusive bongo visit the Ark's waterhole. Next, spend a day at a game ranch between the Aberdare Mountains and Mt. Kenya before heading to Samburu National Reserve, from which you'll take a series of game drives. Cross the equator and stay overnight at Sweetwaters Tented Camp before your journey to Lake Elementeita via Nyahururu Falls. Here the emphasis is on small game and birds such as flamingo and breeding pelicans. After four days investigating the Maasai Mara Reserve and its incredible scenery and big game, the trips heads back to Nairobi. The two-week trip offers one of the more unique itineraries we've seen in East Africa.

Rascals has certainly expanded. They now offer year-round departures to individual families to Costa Rica, Australia and New Zealand, while a June *Family Week* heads to the Galapagos. As we go to press, Theresa and Debby are putting together *Family Week* nature trips to Dominica, Grenada and St. Kitts in the Caribbean. They're pleased that these trips will be more moderately-priced, so that more families will be able to consider them.

PRICES: Rascals price guidelines (land only, generally all-inclusive) are based on a family of four, two adults and two children 2 to 11. Both the

Papua New Guinea and Africa trips range from $8,890 to $11,990; Costa Rica from $4,760 to $5,260, a 12-night Galapagos trip is about $7,100 for a family of three.

PRIMARILY FOR: With the exception of Papua New Guinea, Africa and the Galapagos, there are no minimum ages. Papua New Guinea and Africa have a minimum age of 7, the Galapagos, age 5. Grandparents are commonly found on Rascals trips, though the majority of extended families prefer to arrange for a private departure.

BOOKED FOR TRAVEL

Find Demi's Sea Creatures: *An Animal Game Book,* introduces children to a marvelous array of exotic sea life and then invites them to spot a particular specimen amidst the masses. Not simply a spin-off of *Where's Waldo,* this is a book with an integrity of vision and is both artistic and educational. (Putnam & Grosset)

SUPER NATURAL ADVENTURES (SNA)
626 West Pender Street
Vancouver, B.C. Canada V6B 1V9
Phone: 800-263-1600/604-683-5101
Fax: 604-683-5129

PROFILE: Similar in concept to American Wilderness Experience (see page 52), Super Natural Adventures describes itself as "your link to Canada's West, a land filled with spectacular scenery, abundant wildlife, exciting cities, fascinating culture and history and vast areas of wilderness." It specializes in the Canadian provinces of British Columbia, Alberta and the Yukon and its services can include not only the land portion but all transportation needs — train, rail, car and air — at competitive prices. Formed in 1991, the company works with more than 200 suppliers and outfitters offering both packaged and customized trips.

PROGRAMS: Among SNA's recommendations for families is *Yohetta Wilderness Lodge* in the Chilcotin region of Southern British Columbia. You board a float plane in Whistler, flying over coastal fjords, glaciers, waterfall, rivers and forests en route to Tuzcha Lake where the lodge and its six rustic log cabins with wood stoves await you. Your stay includes two days of guided trail rides, two days of guided hiking, use of fishing gear, canoes, windsurfers, laser boat and lakeside sauna. Wildlife viewing opportunities include grizzly and black bear, cougar, moose, mountain goat and various birds. Guests dine at the resort's lodge, the hub of activity.

If whales strike your fancy, SNA can arrange a number of appealing three-day/two-night trips: *Killer Whales & Campbell River; Hot Springs & Grey Whales; Victoria & Killer Whales.* Much of the exploration is done via Zodiac raft in areas famous for their wildlife viewing and spectacular scenery. Day trips can also be scheduled.

There are also appealing self-drive options, several done in small guided groups with each family in its own four-wheel drive. A wide variety of winter expeditions, including skiing, are also possible.

PRICES: A five-day/four-night stay at *Yohetta Wilderness Lodge* begins at $983/adult, $759/child; *Whale Watching* trips begin at $33/adult for half-day trips, $52/full-day trips, $175/two-night trips.

BOOKED FOR TRAVEL

Meeting the Whales and **Riding with the Dolphins**, both by Erich Hoyt, are guides to locating and recognizing the many varied species of both mammals. The text is supported throughout by color photos and Pieter Folkens' excellent illustrations. These two Equinox Guides, though officially classified as children's books, in our opinion are equally suitable for the adult reader. (Camden House, Canada)

PRIMARILY FOR: The minimum age at *Yohetta Wilderness Lodge* is 8. All ages are welcomed on the whale watching trips so long as parents feel that children can sit for relatively long periods of time. The suggested minimum age is 5.

TREAD LIGHTLY, LTD. (TLL)
1 Titus Road
Washington Depot, CT 06794
Phone: 800-643-0060/860-868-1710
Fax: 860-868-1718

Jim and Audrey Patterson created TLL because of their desire to experience other natures and cultures and visit "rare and untouched regions of the Earth, then leave them, as close as humanly possible, in the condition we found them, having given its people more than short term financial benefits from our visit." A portion of every dollar they take in goes directly to organizations which are preserving the natural and cultural integrity of the destinations they visit.

TLL organizes a variety of ecotourist excursions, for both the intrepid as well as the tentative traveler, as close as Mexico, Central and South America and as far as Borneo or Mongolia, plus a wide array of customized trips. The group size averages about 10 people.

PROGRAMS: TLL considers Costa Rica, Belize and the Galapagos to be "wonderful nature experiences for children. " Two options are offered on the trip to Belize, where, on both, the first four days are spent at Ambergris Cay in the town of San Pedro. The famous barrier reef is located less than half a mile off shore and snorklers and divers alike are enchanted by the incredible coral formation and never-ending parade of colorful fish and marine life. Stopping briefly at Belize City, one option travels to Lamanai Outpost Lodge to board a river boat for the remainder of the trip, heading inland to the New River Lagoon. While staying in the middle of the jungle, you'll paddle a canoe, enjoy an evening safari boat tour and a scenic jungle hike. The second option travels to Western Belize, stopping at the famous Belize Zoo, the Mayan ruins of Xunantunich, visiting the Mountain Pine Ridge Reserve, exploring the natural coves and caves in the area. Both sound incredibly appealing.

TLL sent us a copy of a customized itinerary prepared for a family of five: two parents, two 7-year-old twins and a teenage son. The parents also brought along a nanny for their five-week expedition in South America, which visited Ecuador, Peru, Argentina, Brazil and Guatemala. With the exception of the third week, which was spent at an apartment hotel in Buenos Aires, the trip generally avoided urban areas. Though few of us have the time to enjoy an excursion of such great length, it's obvious that TLL put enormous time and effort into the planning of its itinerary. A nice balance of active and leisure time was combined with numerous cultural and nature-oriented outings. Arrangements included not just private guides, hotel bookings, restaurant reservations and the like, TLL went so far as to coordinate baggage storage for the family when they headed for the Galapagos. In this case, the parents had done lots of homework and had a very clear idea of what they wanted to see and do. Though no specific arrangements were made because of the children, all of the guides and lodgings were told of the kids' ages and interests in advance of their arrival. The trip was considered a great success by all.

PRICES: The Belize trips start at $1,195/adult, including air from the U.S.. Children's prices are determined on a lodge by lodge basis but are usually offered when youngsters share parents' accommodations.

PRIMARILY FOR: Children as young as 8 or 9 have successfully traveled with TLL on its organized departures. Parents should be confident that children can comfortably walk one mile. Younger children can also be considered, especially on customized trips.

CHAPTER 4

ON THE WATER

In your travels, you'd be foolish to restrict yourself to land-based adventures, thereby missing out on all the fascinating opportunities for encountering nature's offerings that are accessible only on the water, whether by raft, canoe, kayak, yacht, cabin cruiser or cruise ship. There's something compelling about experiencing things from the unique vantage point of our planet's varied waterways, where, oftentimes, your group may be the only humans for miles.

BOOKED FOR TRAVEL

The Real Guide: *Able To Travel* is an anthology of experiences of persons with disabilities that range from epilepsy to quadrapeligia. While outdoor trips are not the only ones covered, there are many of these types of experiences included. Most impressive, however, are the myriad lists of resources to whom the disabled can turn to for help. If any family member, or anyone you know, is disabled and wants to travel, this book is certain to give them the confidence to do so. (Prentice Hall)

River rafting is a prime example, and we're not alone in this belief. Canyonlands Field Institute (see page 22) puts it just right: "Rafting is a great way to enjoy the beauty of remote back country and offers a unique floating classroom to study the geology, plants, animals and cultural history." The same is true of all of the options we list in this chapter.

Though rafting is normally considered an adventure trip, not an environmental one, we were surprised to discover that the two went hand-in-hand when we took our first rafting trip with River Odysseys West. On the environmental side, in addition to viewing incredible wildlife — hawks and eagles flying overhead, sheep and deer along the banks, and otter along the river — what the kids learned about care and protection of these pristine surroundings was most impressive. Before we left any site, whether it was a stop for lunch or an overnight, everyone was required to make sure that nothing was left behind, exactly as in the saying — "Take only photos, leave only footprints" — an ethic that we and our kids have retained to this day.

CLASS VI RIVER RUNNERS, INC.
P.O. Box 78
Lansing, WV 25862-0078
Phone: 800-CLASSVI/304-574-0704
Fax: 304-574-4906

PROFILE: In business for 19 years, Dave Arnold, Jeff Proctor and Doug Proctor, managing directors of Class VI, characterize their greatest asset as being able to hear what their guests are looking for. We rafted with them for the first time more than six years ago and have watched them continuously add to and upgrade every aspect of their operation. Fathers themselves, they are thoroughly tuned into the needs of families — offering half price for kids ages 6 to 16 on their one-day trips, providing a playground at their base of operations and arranging childcare for those too young to participate. With raft trips on the New and Gauley Rivers in West Virginia, which pass through the world's oldest mountains, Class VI is as committed to the protection and clean up of the rivers as they are to the sport of rafting. We have so much confidence in Class VI that we sent our own teenage boys and four of their friends for a five-night trip on the New River while we stayed back in the city.

Both the New and Gauley Rivers are part of the largest federally protected watershed in the eastern United States. The gentle upper sections of the New are ideal for family adventures, while the lower section offers incredible whitewater challenges. The Gauley, a dam-controlled river, provides one of the most exhilarating experiences around. We did 10 miles on the Gauley one warm August day when the water level was low enough to use "duckeys," individual rubber kayaks, and learned more about how to read a river than on any other trip we've ever taken. (We were glad we didn't wait, as the next day the river had risen by 10 feet and it was back to multi-person rafts only.) We're looking forward to taking their new *Sunset Cruise* on the New River later this summer, when we're guaranteed to catch the magical, mystical aura this time of day generates.

PROGRAMS: We'll talk more about Class VI's traditional rafting trips in our *Adventure* volume, but suffice it to say that there are trips available for children as young as 6. One of the differences between Class VI and many other river operations is that you don't have to camp along the river (though that is an option), to still get several days of back-to-back rafting under your belt.

For several years, Class VI has been offering both *Birding* and *River Ecology Trips*. Together with our teenager, we joined a one-day ecology trip led by Dr. George Constantz, Director of the Pine Cabin Run Ecological Laboratory, a non-profit organization dedicated to preserving Appalachian rivers. A noted fish ecologist and author of *Hollows Peepers and Highlanders: An Appalachian Ecology*, George is also the father of a soon-to-be teenager and magical with kids. By day's end, we were all able to identify the many different types of trees along the riverfront, learned that only China has similar terrain (a direct result of plate movement millions of years ago), understood the importance of streamside vegetation and had an enormous amount of fun. We were amused when we noticed that some of the teenagers who didn't think it was "cool" to ask questions during George's impromptu talks couldn't resist paddling up close to him later and engaging him in conversation. Today, seven overnight ecology weekends designed-for-families as well as a number of day trips feature Dr. Constantz. The Class VI staff also includes a geologist and an ornithologist. Since these trips will be offered on both the calm upper sections and the challenging lower gorge of the New River, you won't have to sacrifice having an exciting rafting adventure to become more knowledgeable.

Providing one-stop shopping, Class VI can arrange just about every aspect of your stay, beginning with special air fares. They operate a campground and can organize a wide range of lodgings, B&Bs, cabins in state parks or full-service resorts, including The Greenbrier. We encourage you to have at least one meal at Class VI's restaurant, Smokey's Charcoal Grill and to take the Class VI path to the Canyon Rim overlook, with its spectacular view of the New River Gorge and Bridge. Also, be certain to pick up a copy of the video of your trip. You won't be sorry. The New River Gorge National Park Service Visitor's Center is just a five-minute drive and is fun for all ages.

PRICES: A one-day *River Ecology Trip* and the *Birding Trip* on the Upper New are $88/adult, $207 for the two day trip. On the Lower New it's $103/one day, $229/two days. The one-day trips are 50 percent for ages 6 to 16; the two-day trips also offer discounts for the same group.

PRIMARILY FOR: As a general rule of thumb, trips on the Upper New have a minimum age of 6, on the Lower New, 12. However, these age restrictions may be higher on the Lower according to the level of the river and the time of year. Single parents are warmly welcomed and we once rafted with an 80-something year old grandmother with her grandchild!

COASTAL ADVENTURES
P.O. Box 77
Tangier, Nova Scotia, Canada B0J 3H0
Phone/fax: 902-772-2774

PROFILE: It only takes a short conversation with Directors Scott Cunningham and Gayle Wilson of Coastal Adventures, 15 years old in 1996, to recognize their deep commitment to sharing the "unique biology, geology and human history of this fascinating environment" in Atlantic Canada. Equally important for families, they both obviously enjoy having children on their trips.

A former teacher and co-founder of Halifax Field Naturalists, Scott thinks that kids derive particular benefit from the slow and relaxed pace that allows participants to "escape from the routines and pressures of everyday life." As a general rule of thumb, no prior experience is necessary for any of the trips.

PROGRAMS: Coastal Adventures is primarily a sea kayaking operation. The majority of its three- to eight-day trips feature camping, often in remote coves. However, for those not willing to forego the creature comforts, a B&B option, inn-to-inn trips and land-based Nova Scotia nature tours are also offered. Additionally, a *Pedal and Paddle* trip combines three days of cycling with the kayak experience, while one-day land-based *Nature Trips* head into the forest in search of mushrooms during the autumn months.

Atlantic Coastal Islands trips run three, five or seven days in length, paddling through the salt marshes and inlets of Nova Scotia's east coast run from May to October. Five- and seven-day expeditions meander along the northern coast, in the shadow of the Cape Breton Highlands, from June through August. One trip each summer visits Nova Scotia's now deserted easternmost island, Scatarie, as well as Prince Edward Island and Newfoundland.

We're strongly tempted by the three-night trip to the *Bay of Fundy*, where tides can rise as high as 50 feet, winding through a geological wonderland of towering rock formations and sea caves along an ever-changing coastline.

Depending on which trip you select you'll see rocky harbors, salt marshes, glacial ponds, sandy beaches, sea birds, seal colonies, bald eagles or even whales!

PRICES: Prices range from $50 to $995. Family discounts are offered.

PRIMARILY FOR: Tours are most appropriate for children 8 and older. However, we highly recommend speaking with Scott or Gayle prior to making any booking as there is lots of flexibility.

ECHO: THE WILDERNESS COMPANY
6529 Telegraph Avenue
Oakland, CA 94609-1113
Phone: 800-652-3246/510-652-1600
Fax: 510-652-3987

PROFILE: ECHO celebrates its 25th anniversary in 1996, still faithful to its original mission—"To run the highest quality river trips possible: safe, well organized, exciting adventures that promote a greater appreciation of wilderness and wild rivers, and that offer special meaningful experiences for all involved."

Growth came quickly to ECHO in the early years; too rapidly, they decided, when founders Dick Linford and Joe Daly realized that they were operating trips on 18 rivers in five states and two countries. Retrenching, Joe and Dick handpicked what they considered to be the five rivers that would best fulfill their goals. Today, the company offers trips on the Middle Fork and Main Salmon Rivers in Idaho, the Rogue River in Oregon and the Tuolumne and South Fork of the American River in California. Two trips to Alaska are also featured.

Like many raft operators whose brochures extol the joys of rafting for families, ECHO's goes so far as to devote two pages to comments from 10-year-old Meghan who, after her first day on the river, wrote in her diary, "I've never had so much fun." In addition to her remarks on the rafting itself, the excitement it generated, and the astounding sky that greeted her nightly, she added: "On some afternoons, the guides led group hikes along the shore. Tommy and I saw a family of river otters playing, and another time we saw bald eagles. Yesterday, Laura took us to see an old cabin with a bunch of old stuff inside. We could see how people lived a long time ago. On the way back to camp we saw some bear tracks. I can't believe how many different kinds of animals live here."

PROGRAMS: Kids are welcome on all of ECHO's trips. Special *River Trips for Kids* and their parents have scheduled departure dates on the Main Salmon, Rogue and South Fork of the American Rivers. On these trips a *Fun Director* plans exciting activities, from finding crawdads and hunting for animal tracks to stargazing and congregating around the campfire.

To celebrate its anniversary, a new *Natural History Program* will be introduced this summer on two Salmon River itineraries accompanied by a veteran naturalist guide. The Salmon River is the longest undammed river in the continental U.S. and courses through remarkable and varied terrain, from steep, rocky forests to wide open canyons. Keep your eyes peeled for big horn sheep, deer, bear and eagles. There is no mandatory requirement for kids or adults to join in any of the naturalist's special activities, but if you do, you'll come home having learned more about the American wilderness than you ever did in school.

PRICES: Youth rates are valid for ages 7 to 17. The two- to five-day *River Trips for Kids* range from $230 to $915/adult and $220 to $790/youth. The five-day/four-night *Natural History Trip* is $895/adult, $770/youth.

PRIMARILY FOR: The minimum age is 7. Multigenerational groups are often found on the river with ECHO, as are single parents.

GALAPAGOS NETWORK
7200 Corporate Center Drive
Suite 309
Miami, FL 33126
Phone: 800-633-7972/305-592-2294
Fax: 305-592-6394

PROFILE: Describing their trips as "an inspiring adventure, a true hands-on learning experience," Galapagos Network offers families an up close and personal encounter with the islands' unique and intriguing wildlife. The Galapagos became well known to the West for the first time after Charles Darwin visited in 1835, recorded his findings in *The Voyage of the Beagle* and later used them in formulating his theory of evolution.

In operation since 1990, Galapagos Network sails from the port of San Cristobal to the most interesting islands in the chain. Families are welcome on every cruise. Two or three naturalist guides are on board every sailing, depending upon the size of the group. The *Letty, Eric* and *Flamingo* are luxurious motor yachts, each with 10 cabins with private baths and hot water showers. A larger vessel, the *Corinthian,* accommodates 48 passengers and offers many of the features and comforts of a standard cruise liner — a very large dining room, a large lounge, a second lounge with a big-screen TV and a library and a bar plus a Jacuzzi on deck.

For a more intimate experience, ask about trips on the *Sea Cloud*, a sailing vessel that accommodates eight to 10 passengers. Between November and June, these trips offer special diving expeditions for certified divers who must bring all of their own equipment.

PROGRAMS: Though one imagines that the Galapagos Islands are very remote and difficult to reach, Ecuador is only about a six-and-a half-hour flight from New York, and the gateways of Quito and Guayaquil are in the Eastern time zone; the Galapagos themselves are located in the Central time zone, which for us meant no jet lag. We flew overnight on SAETA, the Ecuadorian airline whose one-class plane provided ample legroom, complimentary drinks and headsets and meals served on linen and china. We spent a day in Quito before taking a 20-minute flight to Guayaquil to catch a plane packed with other tourists for the one-hour flight to San Cristobal. Cathy and Carlos, our twenty-something naturalist guides quickly whisked us from the airport through the little town of Puerto Baquerizo Moreno to board the *Letty*, which was sleek and handsomely appointed as promised. During the next 72 hours we made six land excursions to four of the 10 islands in the Galapagos group.

After dutifully reading about the Galapagos in *The Voyage of the Beagle*, we expected the islands to be arid, with poor vegetation and inhospitable in appearance. Darwin visited during the dry month of September; we were there in January when there is some rainfall. January is summer and we found the weather just right for swimming but not too hot for land exploration. Darwin reported no flowers; we found many plants in bloom, including, on Santa Cruz Island, giant tree-sized cacti with bright orange blossoms.

One might imagine that with its unique ecological environment, the creatures of the Galapagos are universally respected and cherished; however, a small backlash exists among certain locals who resent the way the world reveres the animals, while they are struggling to make a living without anyone caring.

We were also somewhat naive to think that our adventures would be primarily land-based, walking around and looking at wildlife. It turns out that aquatic activities like swimming and snorkeling constitute about half the Galapagos experience during its summer months. Masks and flippers are provided by the ship, though no flotation devices were available. (Bring your own if you're not comfortable in the water.) Snorkeling is done from the shore or over the side of a dinghy, which may or may not have a ladder attached. Though the guides have a very relaxed, "no problem" attitude, we think that children should be good, strong swimmers if they're going to snorkel.

Because we went in their summer, we anticipated smooth sailing but encountered rough seas on two of the three nights. According to the Captain, a few weeks earlier it had been calm going all the way. The most stable and comfortable cabins on the boat are on the upper deck.

Our first stop was at Ochoa Beach on San Cristobal, where sea lions slept peacefully among the rocks along the cliffs surrounding the beach. The sand was white, the water turquoise. Sea turtles, rays, schools of fish and a zebra fish were just a teaser for what was to come. After dinner, we checked out the unfamiliar sky of the Southern Hemisphere and tried to spy the Southern Cross. Early the next morning at Punta Suarez, Hood Island, we spotted marine iguanas, reptiles unique to the Galapagos. Endemic to Hood Island is the Christmas iguana, so-called because of its red and green coloration. Though visitors must remain within the boundaries of marked nature trails, we came within inches of colonies of blue footed boobies, masked boobies with their fluffy white chicks, and even a gull chick in the nest. Frigate birds circled above and we encountered sea lions everywhere. There were babies, on their own or nursing, playful youngsters, couples caressing each other with their flippers as they lay sleeping, and thick-necked bulls keeping watch over the herd. We saw the clifftop nesting grounds of the waved albatross. For great wildlife viewing, this was the high point.

The next morning we dropped anchor at Charles Island, commonly known as Floreana. We landed on a brown sand beach populated with the now-familiar sea lions as well as colorful red and orange Sally Lightfoot crabs. Our guide picked up small hermit crabs and allowed us to handle them, the only time we got to touch an animal. Traveling inland, we came to a brackish lagoon for a glimpse of "the world's pinkest flamingos," in a setting straight out of *Jurassic Park*. We also found a secluded beach with the softest, whitest, powder sand imaginable. The turquoise water was calm and inviting, deceptively so, since off shore the ocean harbored an aggressive species of sting ray. We stuck to the beach, enjoying its sea turtle nests and shy coral-colored ghost crabs. Off shore we stopped for the best snorkeling of the trip at Devil's Crown, the crater of a sunken volcano, where innocuous whitehead sharks are sometimes seen.

Later, en route to Puerto Ayora on Santa Cruz, a school of dolphin cavorted alongside the ship. From this charming port town we visited the Charles Darwin Research Station where we saw the famous giant land tortoises (including hatchlings) for which the islands were named. The research station was fairly primitive, with mostly written and pictorial displays with a few enclosures for the tortoises. Much to our chagrin, as on the rest of the trip, this was a hands-off encounter, though we did pose for photos.

When we returned to San Cristobal we noticed that the animals, living closer to civilization, were more leery of people. If we ever get back there, we'll try to visit other islands, including those with active volcanos, penguins or fur seals.

Though there were kids on our trip, there are no special children's activities or youth counselor. Children join all of the shore excursions and particularly enjoy the free time that is given to snorkeling and exploring the beaches during the afternoon.

PRICES: Children 7 to 11 pay 50 percent of the quoted rate (except Christmas, New Year's and Easter weeks). Prices on the *Letty* start at $700/three-night cruise, $900/four-night cruise, and $1,600/seven-night cruise, double occupancy. Seven-night cruises on the *Corinthian* start at $1,100/person for a quad, $1,275/triple, $1,375/double; four nights cost $625 and $800 respectively, three nights $475 and $575.

Extra charges include entrance fees to national parks which cost about $80/person (half price for children under twelve), a new municipal tax of $42/person, a departure tax of $25 and charges for drinks on board the ship.

BOOKED FOR TRAVEL

For the beach and the great outdoors come the **Beach Book** and the **Bug Book**, each of which is accompanied by a plastic specimen container with breathable lid. These are illustrated field guides with suggested activities for young collectors. A younger child will enjoy learning to recognize various creatures encountered through the pictures and an older one can read and absorb all the relevant scientific data about his/her finds. Easy to pack in a suitcase or a child's carry-on, they make ideal traveling companions. (Workman)

PRIMARILY FOR: Children under 7 are not accepted on most sailings unless special arrangements have been made (5 is the absolute minimum age). September to November are prime months for wildlife viewing, though the water is too cold for swimming without a wetsuit; January to April are best for snorkeling and diving. Our guides said that May is their favorite month.

PREMIER CRUISE LINES: THE BIG RED BOAT
400 Challenger Road
Cape Canaveral, FL 32920
Phone: 800-327-7113/407-783-5061

PROFILE: Few cruise lines cater more to children than Premier, which boasts that it has the greatest number of youth counselors in the cruise industry. There are activity programs on its two ships, the *Starship Atlantic* and the *Starship Oceanic*, for five different age groups: *First Mates* (2 to 4); *Kids Call* (5 to 7); *Star Cruisers* (8 to 10); *Navigators* (11 to 13); and *Teen Cruisers* (14 to 17). Each group has a separate playroom; teens have their own night club with state-of-the-art video, light and audio equipment and karaoke. The programs run from 8:30 or 9 a.m. until 10 p.m. at night after which group babysitting is offered in Pluto's Playhouse. Children 2 and older can stay a few hours or even overnight at the cost of $4/hour/first child, $2/hour/each additional child. There's also a kids' supervised dinner on the night of the Captain's cocktail party.

As one would expect, high chairs and booster seats are readily available in the non-smoking dining room, there are cribs upon request and a good number of family suites and five-bedded cabins, plus lots of cabins with bathtubs (something parents of very young children appreciate). Each ship has two outdoor pools with sliding glass roof, a supervised kids' splash pool outside Pluto's Playhouse, a fitness center and televisions in the cabins. Though the ships are quite similar, the *Oceanic's* cabins are about 25 percent larger and the ship has been more recently refurbished. *Looney Tunes* characters (Bugs Bunny, Daffy Duck, Sylvester, et. al.) make special appearances on each sailing, and for an extra fee, there are character breakfasts and bedtime tuck-in visits. We can't stress too much how helpful it is for both parents to attend the *Parent Orientation Talk* which is held shortly after boarding. In addition to hearing about the kids' programs you can find out about evacuation procedures, where to rent strollers, find diapers, and the like.

PROGRAMS: Three- and four-night cruises depart year-round from Port Canaveral, Florida to the Bahamas, docking at Nassau (from which you can opt to visit Salt Cay, Premier's private island) and Port Lucaya.. Cruises can be combined with a three- or four-night vacation at Walt Disney World. The Bahamas is a paradise for anyone who loves the world beneath the sea and many of the Big Red Boat's shore excursions give passengers the chance to get right up close to its inhabitants. There are dolphin encounters both at the UNEXSO facility (see page 44) on Port Lucaya and at Salt Cay. Salt Cay served as the shooting location for many episodes of "Gilligan's Island," and is a true island paradise where the palm trees grow in groves (with ample hammocks for all comers) and there is a warm and shallow lagoon, gentle enough for a baby. Older kids love the pirate treasure hunts, beach olympics and crab racing there. There's a *Splashdown Snorkeling* program at both Salt Cay and Port Lucaya for beginners and intermediates age 8 and older.

Even if you don't want to get wet, there are several ways to enjoy the marvels of these tropical waters. In Nassau, choose between *Coral Island* or a glass bottom boat tour, and in Port Lucaya, go for a ride on the *Seaworld Explorer Semi-Submarine* while seated a mere five feet below the water, or take the plunge in a *DeepStar Submarine*. If your child doesn't want to tear him or herself away from the on-board fun, no problem — the clubhouses are open even in port. However, the kids' programs will also be in full swing ashore; there's a children's room on Port Lucaya and a day's worth of waterfront activities, from pirate treasure hunts to beach olympics, on Salt Cay.

Premier's recently instituted *Voyages of Discovery* is an interactive multi-media experience that's designed to expand the horizons and tickle the fancy of the whole family at once. There are four separate Caribbean-themed programs: *The Sea, The Sky, The Great Ships* and *The History*. Learn where waves come from, where fish fit into the food chain, and what lies above and beyond our planet in the great galaxies that we see only as twinkling stars. Two or three of these programs are scheduled during each cruise. In addition to informative films introduced by a live host, there's all sort of audience participation from a game show to dressing up as your favorite fish.

We've been lucky enough to sail with Premier a couple of times over the last ten years. They really do understand how to please cruisers of all ages. Even though there are often more than 500 children on board, the ships can accommodate them readily. The best part is that it still feels like there's plenty of space and calm for adult passengers.

PRICES: In high season, air included: three-night cruise: $639 to $1,199/adult, $529/child. Four-night cruise: $739 to $1,329/adult $569/child. *Single Parent* and *Family Reunion* fares are available.

PRIMARILY FOR: All ages are actively catered to. No minimum age for baby, but remember, there's no individual babysitting and a child must be 2 to participate in group programs.

RIVER ODYSSEYS WEST, INC. (ROW)
REMOTE ODYSSEYS WORLDWIDE, INC. (ROW)
P.O. Box 579
Coeur d'Alene, ID 83816
Phone: 800-451-6034/208-765-0841
Fax: 208-667-6506

PROFILE: Prior to founding ROW in 1979 with two used rafts, a school bus, and an inordinate love of the river, Peter Grubb worked as a river guide for several years. Today, ROW offers trips on nine rivers in Idaho, Oregon and Montana, warehousing their more than 50 rafts and 10 buses in Clarkston, Washington, while running their sales operation from Coeur d'Alene, Idaho. Internationally, they offer yachting tours along the coast of Turkey, nature-oriented rafting trips in Ecuador and barging along the canals of France. Their newest program, trekking in Nepal, is not water-based.

Peter and his wife Betsy Bowen are parents of two young children, Mariah, 5, and Jonah, 2. Mariah began exploring the river with her parents the summer before her first birthday.

ROW was among the first outfitters to offer family river trips. The company currently operates four or five *Family Focus* trips each summer for children as young as 5, as well as several *ParenTeen Fun* departures.

PROGRAMS: We know first-hand how much fun and how rewarding ROW's *Family Focus* trips are. In fact, one of these was our first river-rafting experience, on which we were joined by another two-parent/two-child family, three single mothers and their sons and five sundry adults, for five days of unending excitement. We were mesmerized every inch of the way on our Salmon River trip, which passed through Hell's Canyon into the Snake River before coming to an end. Eagles soared overhead, sheep and deer grazed along the shores and river otters frolicked as we floated past. One evening, the five boys (ages 7 to 10) spent several hours digging in the sand, trying to replicate a rapid out of twigs, stones and water for their toy plastic kayak.

This *Salmon River Canyons* trip is Peter's top choice for families with young children and we hasten to concur. It's perfect as a combination rafting and camping experience for first-timers. We especially liked the wide sandy beaches where we slept under the stars each night (it was so beautiful we never set up the tents). Fortunately, with the exception of one evening when we were beset by flying, biting ladybugs (quickly and easily controlled with a spritz of bug spray), we didn't encounter any bugs. We were continuously surprised by the quality and quantity of food that was served each and every mealtime — fresh fruit, freshly baked cakes at dinner and other treats. We never felt rushed, and by the second day, our ears were perked, listening for the next rapid.

Three- to five-night *Salmon River Canyons* trips are run from July through September. ROW's brochure lists many other domestic options and gives age guidelines for each of their trips. Trips on U.S. rivers generally run from May to September and hiking/rafting-supported trips are also scheduled.

We're hoping to join *Raft Ecuador* trip (the minimum age is 14 and some rafting experience is recommended). Two itineraries are possible: *River of the Sacred Waterfalls* and *Wings & Whitewater*.

River of the Sacred Waterfalls, an 11-day/10-night trip spending six days and five nights on the river, cuts through the Amazon Basin, home to more than 1,500 species of birds, butterflies galore, and hundreds of mammal, reptile, amphibian and fish species in a veritable botanical garden. During this thrilling journey along the Rio Upano on rubber rafts you'll learn about rain forest ecology of the equatorial ecosystem. The route alternates between wide valleys and narrow canyons, with time for floating and a good share of class II, III and IV rapids. Stop along the way to visit with the Shuar Indians in their palm-thatched huts, camp along sandy beaches and join nocturnal explorations of the jungle. The trip begins and ends in Quito, driving along the "Avenue of the Volcanoes" and overnighting in Banos before arriving at your put-in point of the river. The second night is spent in a small, modest hotel and then it's river time, a day and a half of leisurely floating through the jungle before entering a spectacular gorge and narrow canyon as the river begins to increase in volume. After a final night of camping, it's a bumpy four-hour ride to back to Maca for another modest hotel night. The following day, board a flight to Quito for a hot shower and celebration dinner. A six-day land extension visiting market towns and Inca ruins can follow.

Wings & Whitewater, offered December through March and July and August, is a lodge-based trip that rafts the Rio Blanco and Rio Toachi on the Pacific side of the Andes. Guests meet in Quito on Sunday and head to the Toachi River for three days of whitewater, overnighting at the famous bird-watching resort of Tinalandia in the middle of the rain forest. Wednesday's leisurely-paced sightseeing terminates at the cloud forest of Mindo where El Carmelo de Mindo is your lodge for the next three nights. Thursday and Friday are spent on the Rio Blanco, steeper and faster than the Toachi, with an almost constant succession of class III and IV rapids. Late Friday afternoon the group returns to Quito for a gala farewell dinner. Again, you can return home on Saturday or extend your visit in Ecuador.

PRICES: Youth prices are for kids 16 and younger. Five-day *Salmon River Canyons* trips are $920/adult, $795/youth plus 8 percent tax. *River of the Sacred Waterfalls* is $1,750 with a $100 discount for youths; *Wings & Whitewater* is $850/adult, $650/youth sharing with parents. The five-day/five-night *Market Towns and Inca Ruins* extension is $800/adult, $650/youth.

PRIMARILY FOR: The *Family Focus* trips are primarily for families with children between 5 and 12 years old; *ParenTeen Adventures* for ages 13 to 17. Two to three trips each season span both age groups for those who have children in both age brackets. For Ecuador, teen-agers should have rafting and camping experience. On the *Family Focus* trips about 20 percent are multigenerational groups.

BOOKED FOR TRAVEL

Exploring Europe by Boat: *A Practical Guide to Water Travel in Europe*, by Barbara Radcliffe Rogers and Stillman Rogers, touches briefly on life aboard large cruise ships, but is most helpful in setting out the details of ferry services, harbor tours, trips on classic vessels, etc. The authors feel that traveling by water is a great way to introduce kids to Europe and among the recommended land excursions you'll find many suggestions that will interest kids. (Globe Pequot)

TEMPTRESS VOYAGES
1600 NW LeJeune Road
Suite 301
Miami, FL 33126
Phone: 800-336-8423/305-871-2663
Fax: 305-871-2657

PROFILE: Based in Costa Rica, Temptress markets itself as a "unique eco-adventure cruise sailing the country's celebrated Pacific coast." Owned and operated by Costa Ricans, the Temptress experience was one of the best vacations we've ever taken. It was all it promised to be — and more.

PROGRAMS: In 1995 Temptress inaugurated a *Family Voyages in Costa Rica* program that promised to "delight family members of all ages and interests, from toddlers, youngsters and teens to parents and grandparents." Though our sailing had no toddlers on board, all of the other age groupings were represented and all had a fabulous trip. We opted for the six-night voyage, though two versions of a three-night trip are also offered. We weren't sorry. In spite of the fact that it was rainy season, and we often had choppy seas at night, all of us definitely could have spent a few more days enjoying this small slice of paradise.

It's hard to pinpoint exactly what made this such a superlative journey. Certainly the itinerary, which included visiting a different national park or rain forest every morning followed by a leisurely afternoon and evening more than lived up to our expectations. The ship was not luxurious in its appointments, but it was more than comfortable with surprisingly good food and an unfailingly friendly and helpful crew, even though many of its members spoke little English. Each cabin had two comfortable single beds, a sink and a bathroom with a shower, plus a double window looking out on the sea. Maybe it was Lynn

Gardner, the designated head of the children's program, who was so beloved by all of the children that they hung out in her cabin. Perhaps it was our knowledgeable guides, Mario, Jose and Tony, who so willingly shared their stores of information with us, with such incredible patience for children that we were all a bit overwhelmed. It might have been the numerous choices we had each day — beginning with three morning hikes to select from (one specifically designed to be fun and doable for the kids), to lazing on a beach, scuba diving, heading out in a kayak, visiting a local market or town, doing more hiking, and so on, each afternoon. We especially liked the service that took our laundry each day and returned it the next, clean and folded. When you put it all together, it adds up to one terrific week. This is a remarkably easy trip for families. It is truly all-inclusive (except for tips and a few personal items). Lynn's caring for the children extended well beyond planning and taking them on hikes they would enjoy (on one trip she told us that she carried an 18-month-old much of the time), but her vigilant attitude on shore was more than admirable. She knew exactly where each child was and which parents were watching (she was certain to keep her eagle eyes and those of other crew members on the rest), ensuring the safety of all. After each wet landing (and most were pretty wet) finding clean towels to wipe one's feet before putting shoes back on was just one of the special touches provided for passengers. Also appreciated were the pre-peeled oranges and ice-water canteens to scoop up before going ashore, fresh guava and other juices at the end of each hike and the cleaning and drying of shoes after returning to the ship.

The casual atmosphere helped also. There was no dressing for dinner, no worrying about whether the kids would like the food (there was always something very child-friendly served and fresh fruit is abundant), no lines to wait in, no reservations to make. The guests were interesting and eclectic — families of all types, honeymooners, seniors and young athletic types — none of whom complained about having kids on board. Though the hikes required waking up early — some departed as early as 6:30 a.m. — only our teenager chose to sleep in one day. We were all, old hands and novices alike, enchanted and energized by our hikes, which suited both the more intrepid and more sedentary in the group. Family members could hike together, separately or not at all, without worrying about each other. In the evenings we talked, played games (often joined by crew members), heard about the naturalist's children and learned a lot about the country of Costa Rica, Central America's long-time safe haven.

The six-night trip begins at San Jose Airport (we flew American from Miami; LACSA, the airline of Costa Rica also offers scheduled service from several U.S. cities) followed by an approximately two-hour scenic bus trip to the port of Puntarenas, where the ship is docked.

We took a side trip to *The Butterfly Farm* in Monteverde which we initially thought would bore the kids. Were we ever wrong. We spent almost two hours there and were all engaged. The threat of the ship departing without us was the only incentive we had to leave. We highly recommend that you take the time to watch the short video before actually visiting the garden. By the time we entered the relatively small butterfly enclosure, we felt like experts and knew and understood what we were observing. It turns out that *The Butterfly Farm* is a major exporter of butterflies to museums and botanical gardens around the world.

Once on the ship, we soon learned that the rainy season doesn't necessarily mean that it rains all day (and it never did) but that you are pretty much guaranteed that it will rain a little (or a lot) each day. The first evening, and each evening that follows, guests and staff meet in the comfortable, air-conditioned lounge to talk about the following day and watch some slides. We brought along the "Travelers Notebook" from our cabin, a field log listing all of the different birds, mammals, amphibians, reptiles and plants likely to be encountered during our outings. For the kids, there was a very nicely designed travel journal/coloring book to help familiarize them with Costa Rica.

A relatively short four-hour overnight sail from the port of Puntarenas took us to Curu, home to the Curu Biological Reserve. Morning hikes were followed by a delightful afternoon on Tortuga Island. After dinner on the beach or on board, there was a long (and, for us, pretty rocky) journey to Corcovado National Park, considered Costa Rica's crown jewel and home to some of the more spectacular wildlife seen on the trip. Then it was on to Drake Bay, where the banana boat took the kids (and adults) for rides, the waterski boat was ready to go. Lots of folks kayaked up the river while others stayed ashore to watch the sunset over the Pacific. Some of the children and their parents went to visit the local school with Tony, our guide who came from those parts. By now everyone was in heaven. Next day, we took a visit to one of the country's most popular national parks, Manuel Antonio. Here, the indigenous wildlife is much more accustomed to humans than at Corcovado, making them in some ways easier to spot, but in other ways more leery.

Another day, we returned to a different section of Corcovado National Park. It was on this occasion we spotted the howler monkeys mentioned in the *Introduction*. We had waited all week to see these rare simians, but were somewhat intimidated when, upon realizing we were there, they began to throw branches at the unwelcome intruders. In spite of this, it was all very exciting and all the kids couldn't stop talking about the incident for the rest of the day.

On our final day, some of the guests headed on their own for the notable rain forest canopy of the Carara Biological Reserve. We, unfortunately, had to return to the airport to catch our flight home. There's much more we'd like to do in Costa Rica. Several of our fellow seafarers had spent time on land prior to boarding the *Temptress,* all with glowing reports of their various adventures. We met a couple from Arizona who spent a week with Elderhostel (see page 31), a California family with two teens who'd been scuba diving on the Caribbean side of the country, and California grandparents and their two young grandchildren who seemingly visited everywhere else. We saw enough to understand the great appeal of Costa Rica, enough to know that we will definitely return. Though we'd like to go when it's not rainy season, there were advantages to going when we did. After the rain, the birds of the forest spread their wings to dry them in the sun and such a spectacular sight is hard to match.

Temptress Voyages has grown. As of February '96, the ship we sailed with is now sailing off the coast of Belize. The Belizian journey is similar in design to the trip to Costa Rica with one six-night and two three-night options. There's a real mix of land and sea in the itinerary and, if you're a scuba diver, you'll be all set. The stops include Goff's Caye, Manatee Beach/Rendezvous Caye, Sittee River/Bird's Caye, Tobacco Caye/Placencia, Monkey River/Laughingbird Caye, Snake's Caye/Punta Gorda, with a final optional visit to Altun Ha. Friends of ours recently took this cruise and loved it, even though it was once again during rainy season which resulted in many fewer water activities than originally scheduled. As with our trip in Costa Rica, this didn't stop the Temptress folks who managed, often at the last minute, to plan exciting and exhilarating daily excursions. A family program will also operate during the summer months.

PRICES: Costa Rica: From June to September, prices start at $795/adult/double and $495/child for three-night trip; $1,495/adult/double and $895/child for six-night trip. *Belize:* From May to October, prices start at $695/adult/double and $350/child for three-night trip; $1,290/adult/double and $500/child for six-night trip.

PRIMARILY FOR: On summer family trips, all ages are welcome, from toddlers to teens on up through senior family members.

CHAPTER 5

DESTINATIONS

Family travel encompasses such a vast diversity of interests that it's highly unlikely each and every vacation you take will put you smack in the midst of the wilderness. In fact, there's a good possibility that most of your trips will be to destinations that are sure-fire kid-pleasers, offering a combination of indoor and outdoor fun for all.

This chapter features 10 such destinations, some of which may surprise you since, by most standards, they don't seem to qualify as *Nature Vacations*. On closer examination, however, you'll see that each of our choices affords a wealth of nature-oriented outings to enhance the vacation experience. For each destination, we give you a selection of daily excursions which we hope will inspire you to strike out and explore the surrounding environs.

You may decide to stay at a local full-service resort or opt for a more budget-friendly accommodation and put your money into the excursions. The choice is yours and *BEST BEDS* will help steer you in the right direction.

WEST

ARIZONA: PHOENIX
Phoenix & Valley of the Sun Convention & Visitors Bureau
One Arizona Center
400 E. Van Buren Street, Suite 600
Phoenix, AZ 85004-2290
Information: 602-254-6500

Unless otherwise stated, the area code is 602.

PROFILE: Phoenix lies in the heart of the Valley of the Sun, surrounded by mountain ranges on all four sides. The Hohokam Indians, who dwelt here from 300 to 1450 AD before they mysteriously disappeared, built a series of canals to irrigate their fields, which stretched out into the Sonoran Desert. (You can see some of these from the top of the Casa Grande Ruins National Monument in Coolidge, phone 520-723-3172.) The average daytime temperature in the Valley is a comfortable 72 degrees, though it can soar into the hundreds come summer.

Phoenix is a blend of the old west and modern-day urban sophistication, and while more visitors come for its golf courses than for the spectacular scenery, there are choices galore for those who want to experience the surrounding desert environs first-hand. When you head out into the desert, be prepared. Wear long pants, leather (not cloth) shoes, know what jumping cholla cacti look like (in order to avoid them), and don't trample on the underbrush as many plants have shallow root systems. Protect yourself and your kids from the sun by wearing a hat, sunglasses and sunblock. Always travel with plenty of water: the desert rule recommends one gallon per person per day. Above all, never wander too far from your car.

PLACES: Begin exploring nature right in the city at **South Mountain Park** (495-0222), the largest municipal park in the world, its many hiking trails include one that passes through a natural tunnel. Pick up a map at the gatehouse and ask about the desert awareness programs. South of the Phoenix Zoo (see below) lies the **Salt River Project History Center** (236-2208 or 236-5451), which offers hands-on exhibits demonstrating the use of water through the ages.

If it's animal encounters you seek, **Out of Africa Wildlife Park** (837-7779) in Fountain Hills, which is neither a theme park nor an animal park, should be on your itinerary. Owned and operated by Dean and Bobbi Harrison, it houses big cats: lions, tigers, panthers and cougars among them. While there are nine daily shows, no one ever quite knows what to anticipate since the cats are not trained and the shows are really playtimes for man and cat. There are other animals as well as a small petting area. Move quickly if you see a cat getting ready to urinate — the stream can flow as far as 20 feet! Expect to spend the better part of a day here.

Located in Papago Park, the **Phoenix Zoo** (273-1341) is the largest non-profit zoo in the country. Its more than 1,300 animals (many on the endangered list) live in habitats designed to recreate their natural environment, e.g., the Sonoran Desert, a simulated tropical rain forest, an African savanna, monkey islands and more.

Next to the Zoo, the **Desert Botanical Garden** (941-1217) is filled with plants that grow in arid regions of the globe. At the *Center for Desert Living* you'll find a working research facility and at *Desert House* an exhibit of ecological ways to save energy. If you think only cacti thrive in this environment, you're in for a surprise. Spring brings an explosion of color to the desert, and during March and April the Garden has a **Wildflower Hot Line** (481-8134) telling what's blooming where.

Arizona's largest collection of exotic animals is on view at **Wildlife World Zoo** (935-WILD) in Litchfield Park. The more than 2,000 animals include llamas, camels, birds and reptiles.

Strike out for the desert with **Arizona Awareness Desert Jeep's** (947-7852) half- or full-day natural history tours, gold panning trips or customized outings. Nigel Reynolds of **Backroad Adventure** (510-5626) will transport you and your kids (under 14, free) by Land Rover to his favorite regions of the desert, but he makes it clear that the trip is yours, not his! **Apache Trail Tours** (982-7661) hurtles down a harrowing wilderness road, part of which was once the major thoroughfare of the Apache Indians, out to the **Theodore Roosevelt Dam**. In Apache Junction, you can take an underground mine tour at **Goldfield Ghost Town and Mine Tours** (983-0333). Additional options include a sunset tour and a combination helicopter/jeep ride. **Old West Trails'** (488-9541) jeep tours concentrate on history and desert ecology. Children under 12 ride for half price. Participants out at **Cowboy Adventures** (377-8281) shed their city slicker image as soon as they don genuine cowpoke garb. Located on the Fort McDowell Indian Reservation (not far from Out of Africa), trail rides, wild west rides, jeep tours, even an overnight stay, are all possible (best for children 6 and older). One of the newest kids on the block to offer wilderness tours with a twist is **Desert Storm Hummer** (922-0020).

Further afield, **Arcosanti** (520-632-7135), 60 miles north of the city, is the 23-years-in-the-making vision of architect Paolo Soleri, now in his 70s. This prototype "arcology" development celebrates the marriage of ecology and architecture. Try to be there for a silt sculpture workshop which welcomes ages 6 to adult. One 13-year-old we know described it as "a work in progress, a model for the city of the future. It was amazing and beautiful in a strange, futuristic way."

Llama Hikes of Arizona (800-899-7356/399-0664) can refer you to outfitters in the state that arrange trips with these pack animals. Joyce and John Bittner, the organizers of this service, also run **Fossil Creek Llamas** (520-476-4908) which offer everything from hiking for a few hours in the forest to overnight trips, camping either in the wilderness or in their "private" forest. Elk, deer, coyote and many varieties of bird provide the backdrop to your trip to the Strawberry area, about 100 miles northeast of Phoenix at 6,000 feet.

BEST BEDS: The Valley of the Sun offers families a remarkable number of lodging options: B&Bs, All-Suite Hotels, Resorts, Motels, Campgrounds/RV Resorts and Apartment/Condominium Rentals. The *Official Visitor's Guide* (available from the tourist office listed above) offers a prodigious listing. The tourist office can also send a copy of its brochure, *Affordable Accommodations.*

Many resorts in the area feature activity programs for children. In fact, the program at the Hyatt Regency at Gainey Ranch was the prototype for the system-wide *Camp Hyatt* program (see page 144). Our kids have spent time in the programs at the Arizona Biltmore and The Point Hilton Resort at Squaw Creek in Phoenix and at the Hyatt Regency and at Mariott's Camelback Inn in Scottsdale.

We've also received good reports on the programs at The Phoenician, the Scottsdale Princess and the Ritz-Carlton.

CALIFORNIA: PALM SPRINGS DESERT RESORTS
Palm Springs Desert Resorts Convention & Visitor's Bureau
69-930 Highway 111
Rancho Mirage, CA 92270
Information: 800-41-RELAX/619-770-9900

Unless otherwise stated, the area code is 619.

PROFILE: In the heart of the arid Colorado Desert is a modern-day oasis, the Palm Spring Desert Resorts. Eight communities comprise the resorts" — Cathedral City, Desert Hot Springs, Indian Wells, Indio, La Quinta, Palm Desert, Palm Springs and Rancho Mirage. Over the years, they have sported diverse images: *Playground of the Stars,* still *Date Capital of the World,* and international golfers' Mecca. Most recently, it has become a family vacation destination where parents can choose among a dozen hotels with top-of-the-line children's activity programs. Another tip off that families are an important factor in regional tourism is the presence of the highly regarded **Children's Museum of the Desert** in Rancho Mirage.

Whatever time of year you visit, you're bound to find a wide and varied array of fun. Temperatures are high (and dry) in summer; winter nights are cool and require jackets. February's *Riverside County Fair & National Date Festival* is a particularly amusing time with its camel and ostrich races and 10 days of on-going entertainment.

When you head out to investigate the desert, we remind you to follow the advice on page 102 regarding special precautions in this environment. If you have a car, we encourage you to take the Palms to Pines Highway #74 to get a bird's eye view of how the desert transforms into the Alpine terrain of the San Jacinto Mountains.

PLACES: By way of introduction, take the 14-minute ride from the desert palms near the center of town up the mountain in the **Palm Springs Aerial Tramway** (325-1391) to Mt. San Jacinto Wilderness State Park, a 13,000-acre Alpine forest. In winter, there's often snow up here and the Nordic Center tries to keep its cross-country trails open through

April. Summer brings guided mule train rides into the park, plus 54 miles of hiking trails.

Palm Desert's **Living Desert Wildlife & Botanical Park** (346-5694) is 1,200 acres filled with many of the world's rarest and most exotic desert animals, from Arabian oryx to zebras. Additionally there are six miles of nature, geology and hiking trails and a botanical garden with more than 15,400 varieties of plant life, representing 10 different regions in North America and Africa. During March and April, there's a hotline (340-0435) that directs visitors to the places where the desert wildflowers are in bloom. The facility is closed in August.

Palm Springs Desert Museum (325-7186) focuses on art, the natural sciences and the performing arts. Believing that "to comprehend nature is to nourish the soul," visitors learn which native animals live and survive by day and which are nocturnal. You can also check out "earthquake country" and the nearby San Andreas Fault. From November through April *Nature Field Trips & Treks* are led by museum naturalists, some of which are ideal for families.

Don't miss **Hot Springs Park** (329-6411) in Desert Hot Springs, whose bubbling, hot mineral waters made the area famous. Parents and kids both enjoy visiting the new interpretive center that features hot and cold water and a mini-grove illustrating how water is used in the desert.

Again, not to be missed are **Palm Spring Indian Canyons** (325-5673), home to the Agua Caliente Band of Cahuilla Indians whose ancestors settled in five canyons — Palm, Murray, Andreas, Tahquitz and Chino — all rich in water, animals and plants. Traces of the communities can still be seen and the area is still considered sacred to its native peoples. Boasting the greatest number of palm trees in the world, Palm, Andreas and Murray Canyons are open for exploration by foot or horseback. A good 15 miles long, Palm Canyon's abundant palm trees stand as a breathtaking contrast to the barren rocky desert lands beyond. Pick up a hiking map at the Trading Post. Magnificent fan palms bloom in the lush oasis of Andreas Canyon. A scenic foot trail passes stately palms and unusual rock formations and is reputed to be great birdwatching terrain. From here it's an easy hike to Murray Canyon, where peninsula big horn sheep still roam. Tahquitz Canyon is blessed with majestic waterfalls and pools and abundant plant and wildlife, and though no entrance is permitted at the present time, there are plans to make it the home of Agua Caliente Cultural Museum.

Palm Spring's only "living museum," **Moorten's Botanical Garden,** dates back to 1938 and harbors 3,000 plants, including giant cacti, in an oasis paradise with scenic nature trails. This "oasis paradise" boasts the world's first "cactarium" plus displays of rocks, crystals and wood formations.

Fully 95 percent of the dates grown in the United States originate in this region. Among the date ranches open to the public are **Oasis Date Gardens** (399-5665) and **Shields Date Gardens** (347-0996).

If your kids are like ours, active and curious, head for the sand dunes at **Off Road Rentals** (375-0376) where you can rent ATVs for self-guided tours on a private desert. Various sized vehicles are possible and are "suited to the age and size" of the rider. Sounds like fun to us.

Another enclave of The Nature Conservancy (see page 40), the **Coachella Valley Preserve** (343-1234) contains 13,000 acres of mesas, bluffs and dunes. The Thousand Palms Oasis is just one of the spectacular sights accessible via the hiking and riding trails.

North of the city in Morongo Valley, **Big Morongo Canyon Preserve and Covington Park** (363-7190) is both an important sanctuary for wild animals of the desert and mountain as well as a prime site for birdwatching. Go for a hike and bring a picnic.

It would take many visits to do justice to the wonders of **Joshua Tree National Park** (367-7511), a huge 1,241 square mile area that encompasses the upper Mojave and lower Colorado Deserts and three distinct ecosystems. In the upper you'll see the famous Joshua Tree, while the lower is dominated by creosotebush and spidery ocotillo and jumping cholla cactus. Fan palms thrive in the oases. A haven for rock-climbers, there are hundreds of varieties of flora and a wildlife sanctuary with coyote, jackrabbit, bobcat, burrowing owl, kangaroo rats, golden eagle, roadrunners and snakes. The Oasis Visitor Center is located in Twentynine Palms.

While you can see most of these spots on your own, there are several folks who are anxious to show you the way. **Desert Adventures** (864-6530), the only wilderness jeep tour company in the area, brings the desert alive for you with fascinating, colorful commentary by expert naturalist guides. Trips visit Indian Canyons, the Santa Rosa Mountains and Mystery Canyon on the San Andreas Fault. **Trail Discovery Hiking Guide Service** (325-HIKE) offers guided hikes in the breathtaking Coachella Valley foothills, all led by professional guides. **Covered Wagon Tours** (347-2161) at the Coachella Valley Preserve has two-hour mule-drawn wagon tours accompanied by knowledgeable desert naturalists who demonstrate how Native Americans used natural plants for food and medicine. Back at camp there's a chuck-wagon cookout. **Ranch of the 7th Range** (777-7777) features two-hour horseback trips into the Preserve. Children must be 4 and older to ride their own horses but younger ones can double up with a parent. A number of bike tours and balloon companies also operate in the area.

BOOKED FOR TRAVEL

The Desert, The Forest, The Ocean and **The River** are all *Nature Panorama* books which illustrate four distinct aspects of the natural world and the flora and fauna that inhabit them. The folding board book format will appeal to a variety of ages, and Susan Deming's drawings are both realistic and charming. (Chronicle)

BEST BEDS: The best descriptions of area lodging for families which we've seen is in *California With Kids, a Frommer Family Travel Guide* by Carey Simon and Charlene Marmer Solomon (Prentice Hall Travel). Their write-ups include low-cost budget to high-price luxury accommodations, including all-suite hotels and condominium rentals.

Among those properties featuring children's programs are the Ritz-Carlton Resort, the Westin Mission Hills Resort and Marriott's Las Palmas Resort & Country Club in Rancho Mirage, Shadow Mountain Resort in Palm Desert, Hyatt Grand Champions and Stouffer Renaissance Esmeralda in Indian Wells and La Quinta Resort in Palm Springs. Recently, the Palm Springs Marquis Crowne Plaza Resort & Suites has added a program for children as young as 2-years-old.

We've visited (alas, without our children) all three of the Rancho Mirage properties and have enjoyed each of them, though they are quite different in ambience. Before booking any of these hotels, ask about the exact ages accepted and dates the children's programs operate as many are seasonal.

HAWAII: MAUI
Maui Visitors Bureau
P.O. Box 580
Wailuku, Hawaii 96793
Information: 800-525-MAUI/808-244-3530

Unless otherwise stated, the area code is 808.

PROFILE: The second largest of the Hawaiian Islands, Maui offers more than its fair share of nature-oriented family fun. Whether you're staying in a West Maui resort between Kaanapali and Kapalua, at the South Maui areas of Kihei, Wailea or Makena, or venturing to the remote Hana in the East, the enchantment of the Valley Isle will linger. We urge you to participate in a luau and taste traditional Polynesian specialties such as poi and poisson cru. If you visit between December and March, be on the lookout for whales, since about 20 percent of the world's humpback whale population winters in these waters, which have recently been designated a cetacean sanctuary. Some say the best whalewatching view is from the scenic lookout at MacGregor Point on the Honoapiliani Highway (on the way to Lahaina), overlooking Maalaea Bay where the whales breed and play. We like the idea of being on the water, which is exactly where we were one January when a pod of whales breached right next to our snorkel boat.

Among the nature-oriented festivals are: *Whalefest,* celebrated in Lahaina in January, includes lots of fun activities including *Whale Discovery Day* at Whalers Village. In March, the Pacific Whale Foundation (879-8811) hosts the *Great Whale Count*, an island-wide event. Other annual events are the *Haiku Flower Festival,* the *Keiki Fishing Derby* and the *Maui Onion Festival.* There are an amazing number of hiking opportunities on Maui; ask for details from the toll-free number above or contact Hike Maui at 879-5270 upon arrival. Serious ecotourists should pick up a copy of David Zurick's *Hawaii, Naturally* (Wilderness Press) or *Adventuring in Hawaii* by Richard McMahon (Sierra Club Books) and purchase *The Maui Eco Directory* (669-4743) an annual brochure cum map that is sold at the Lahaina Visitors Center, Miracles Bookery in Makawao and Aloha Books in Kihei.

PLACES: The whaling village of Lahaina was once the royal capital of the Hawaiian Islands. In the harbor, the **Carthaginian** sailing brig is now a whaling museum (661-3262). Another fun excursion, nearby and on the town's free trolley route is the **Lahaina-Kaanapali & Pacific Railroad** (667-6851), the *Sugar Cane Train,* pulled by a vintage steam engine through the sugar fields. There are numerous whalewatching, snorkeling and scuba options in town. Younger kids might enjoy a glass-bottom boat trip, an excursion on a semi-submersible or even a journey on the **Atlantis Submarine** (667-2224, see page 188).

As you drive up the coast towards Kapalua, stop at **Hobbitland** at Nakalele Point to view gushing geysers and old lava tubes an easy hike from the road. Kapalua is filled with generation-old breadfruit, lychee and mango trees and ginger and ti leaf plants. All three of Kapalua's golf courses are certified Audubon Cooperative Sanctuaries.

Heading away from the shore, Kahului is home to the **Alexander & Baldwin Sugar Museum** (871-8058), which chronicles early plantation life and the history of the sugar industry. At **Maui's Tropical Plantation** (244-7643) near Wailuku, ride a tram through groves of pineapple, macadamia nuts, guava and bananas and then stay on for an evening barbecue.

Further inland, the **Iao Valley,** with its 1,200 foot monolith, beck-ons hikers to strike out among the giant tree ferns and the ti and ohio trees. The **Hawaii Nature Center** (244-6500) supplies free trail maps and guides weekend hikes into the valley. There are many family workshops (geared for different age groups, starting for children as young as 3), among them: *Nature Rovers, Natural Collage, Birds, Bugs and Beasts of Iao,* and *Maui on the Go with H₂0* for teenagers. Reservations are required.

No trip to Maui is complete without visiting **Haleakala National Park** (572-9306) atop Maui's dormant volcano. Two observation houses are located on the crater rim and there are many marked hiking trails. Be certain to check out the park's *Junior Ranger* program for children 5 to 12. The two hours of activities, which earn kids a badge, focus on the area's endangered species and fragile ecosystem. For many, making a pilgrimage to the top of the mountain to watch the sun as it rises from within the volcanic crater is the island's most awesome experience. Bike tours (**Maui Downhill,** 871-2155, minimum age 12, minimum height five feet), horseback rides (**Pony Express Tours,** 677-2202) or helicopter tours (**Sunshine Helicopters,** 871-0722; **Blue Hawaiian Helicopters,** 871-8274) can take you into the vast crater where wildlife and plants found nowhere else on earth thrive. This eerie, moonlike terrain was used as a training ground for American astronauts. There's also a free tour of the 34-acre experimental garden run by the **University of Hawaii** (244-3242). The garden is located on Copp Road in Kula, off of Highway 377, and is closed on Fridays.

Not all tourists are intrepid enough to venture along the notoriously windy *Road to Hana* but, for those who do, the spectacular scenery — waterfalls, plunge pools, fruit trees and taro patches along the rugged lava shore — makes it well worth the effort. In the town of **Hana,** visit the botanical gardens, ride on horseback at Hana Ranch and don't miss the famous cascading **pools** at Kipahulu (they are often erroneously referred to as the Seven Sacred Pools). Follow the signs to Oheo Stream.

Marked trails wind through a bamboo forest to **Waimoku Falls.** Here rangers are constructing replicas of ancient Hawaiian dwellings where there will be demonstrations of the old ways, including poi pounding and basket weaving. The drive-through **Helani Gardens** (248-8274) are well worth a visit, but do leave time to get out of the car.

We've spent most of our visits to Maui staying in **Wailea,** in the shadow of Haleakala. From here we've taken snorkel trips to the

Molokini Crater with **Ocean Activities Center** (879-4485) which also arranged several scuba diving adventures for us. Ocean kayaking is another popular activity in this area.

BEST BEDS: Deciding where to stay on Maui is a mind-boggling exercise as there are so many quality properties from which to choose. Moreover, there are probably more hotels with excellent activity programs for youngsters in most other resort destinations.

Our kids' first choice is the Grand Wailea Resort in Wailea where the 20,000 square foot children's center rivals the resort's other incredible facilities and amenities. The resort's fantastic pool enchants old and young alike. However, the program at the Maui InterContinental, though substantially less grand in its offerings, kept our boys happy and busy on several afternoons and evenings. Also in the Wailea/Makena vicinity, the Stouffer Renaissance Wailea Beach Resort, the Kea Lani Hotel, Suites & Villas and the Four Season Resort offer children's activity programs.

In the Lahaina/Kaanpali area the Maui Marriott, the Hyatt Regency Maui, the Westin Maui, the Royal Lahaina Resort, The Whaler on Kanapali Beach, the Ka'anapali Beach Hotel, and Aston's Maui Kaanapali Villas and Embassy Suites feature activities just for keikis (kids in Hawaiian). The Ritz-Carlton Kapalua, the Kapalua Bay Hotel and the more remote Hotel Hana Maui offer organized children's programs.

BOOKED FOR TRAVEL

The University of Hawaii Press is the best source for good children's books about Hawaii. Some examples: **A is for Aloha** is a classic — a perfect introduction to the delights of a young child's Hawaii. Stephanie Feeney keeps the background information simple, just enough to intrigue a child, while Hella Hammid's black-and-white photos are full of joy and speak volumes in themselves. . . **Sand to Sea, Marine Life of Hawaii,**also by Feeney, along with Ann Fielding, is an outstanding photographic guide for children to the fauna of Hawaii's beaches, tidepools, reefs and oceans. Ed Robinson's color underwater photography is some of the best we've seen. Every bit of the text is interesting and worth reading. There's even a section on hazardous animals, like urchins, Portuguese-men-of-war and cone shells, with instructions on how to treat wounds if accidentally stung... Kids of all ages will enjoy reading (or being read) two delightful stories by Julie Stewart Williams about Maui, Hawaii's best-loved mythical hero: **And the Birds Appeared** and **Maui Goes Fishing** (you'll never guess what he catches).

CENTRAL/ROCKIES

MISSOURI: BRANSON
The Branson Lakes Area Chamber of Commerce
Box 1897
269 West Route 248 at Route 65
Branson, MO 65615
Information: 800-477-2751/417-334-4136

Unless otherwise stated, the area code is 417.

PROFILE: One of the most popular drive-vacation spots in America, Branson is "America's Live Entertainment Capital," the Ozark Mountain town where many entertainers have realized the American Dream. Despite the traffic caused by the more than five million visitors, the general consensus is that Branson is a friendly, fun, affordable and a wholesome family destination. To avoid the congestion, pick up a copy of the *Branson Roads Scholar* map from the Chamber of Commerce and you'll be able to better manoeuver in and out of the traffic.

Though the music may lure you here, plan time to enjoy the area's cool mountain lakes, world-class fishing and natural surroundings. You won't find any better detailed information than in Fodor's *Branson, The Official Travel and Souvenir Guide to America's Music Show Capital*, by Jordan Simon, a savvy and sophisticated born-and-bred New Yorker. Though high season is May through October, when the town is abustle, theaters and many entertainment complexes are open the rest of the year.

Curiously, it was a natural phenomenon, Marvel Cave, that first brought tourists to Branson.

PLACES: Start where it all began, at **Marvel Cave** in **Silver Dollar City** (800-952-6626). Discovered by the Osage Indians in the 1500s, the cave was first opened to tourists in 1894. A Chicago family bought the cave in 1949 and began holding dances in its huge Cathedral Room where the constant temperature of 58 degrees made it a perfect spot on hot summer evenings. Eventually a tram was built to take visitors out of the cave. In 1960 the cave owners recreated an 1880s village around the cave entrance and the rest is history. Today the park features crafts, entertainment and rides and it the largest single tourism-related employer in Ozark Mountain Country. As you might have guessed, limestone caverns are the natural counterpart to the rolling hills and streams above ground and there are many other caverns in the area. **Talking Rocks** (272-3366) is one, a giant room with an incredible array of rock formations, including calcite curtains and an Angel, complete with wings. **Fantastic Caverns** (833-2010), in nearby Springfield, can be viewed while riding a jeep-drawn tram. It's filled with stalactites, soda straws, tiny cave pearls and animals that are able to survive despite the lack of sunlight. At **Cosmic Cavern** (501-749-2298) in Berryville, Arkansas — "Arkansas's most awesomely decorated show cave" — they're still discovering new rock formations. Another spotlight is its gemstone panning spot.

You'll discover lots more to see and do above sea level, too, after viewing *Ozarks, Legacy & Legend,* a dramatization of the history, culture and geography of the area, at the **Ozark Discovery IMAX Theater** (335-4832). Hop on the **Branson Scenic Railway** (334-6110) and head for the Ozark hills on a 40-mile round-trip trek from the center of town. After checking out the *Kewpie Doll Museum* at **Bonniebrook** (561-2250), a National Historic Site with the replicated home (the original was destroyed by fire) of Rose O'Neill, stroll through the flower gardens and enjoy the park's waterfalls along the scenic hiking trails.

Kids who love animals will especially enjoy visiting **Exotic Animal Paradise** (859-2159) in Strafford. Don't miss the baby animal nursery after you drive through the park. Nearby, **Bass Pro Shop's Outdoor World** (800-BASS-PRO), a 150,000 square foot showroom, also features a wildlife center with waterfalls, log cabin, working water wheel plus more than 14,000 retail items. Five miles of interpretative trails around Springfield Lake and hands-on displays are on tap at the **Springfield Conservation Nature Center** (882-4237).

Surrounded by **Mark Twain National Forest**, three major lakes — Taneycomo, Bull Shoals and Table Rock — invite discovery. At the **Dewey Short Visitors Center at Table Rock Lake** (334-4101), learn about the marriage of man and nature on the Powerhouse Dam tour. A number of video presentations, including *The Taming of La Riviere Blanche* and *Ozark Glades,* may also be of interest. A nature trail winding through the woods along the shoreline is open to the public. Just below the dam, along Lake Taneycomo, see the **Shepherd of the Hills Fish Hatchery** (334-4865), a trout-rearing facility operated by the Missouri Department of Conservation. Exhibits, aquaria, guided tours, multimedia presentations, nature trails and fishing are all offered.

Kids can take their turn at the wheel and help navigate your **Ride The Ducks** (334-3825) tour. View the dam, the fish hatchery, Table Rock and more during the hour-long voyage across land and water. At the end of the trip, be sure your kids pick up their "Captain's Certificate." Head out onto the water on your own or with a river guide at **Northfork River Outfitters** (261-2259). Even totally inexperienced families can soon become comfortable in their canoes and kayaks. Canoes, paddle boats, row boats, wave runners and more can all be yours at the **State Park Marina** (334-3069) in Table Rock State Park, where John the Diver can take you to the depths of the lake to see an unusual underwater world. Ozark nature explodes along the gentle springfed stream of Beaver Creek where **Beaver Canoe Rental** (796-2336) can outfit you. They'll also take you to nearby Swan Creek for a whitewater adventure.

Mark Twain National Forest (683-4428) is comprised of 1.5 million acres, 65,000 of which are designated as wilderness, including the Piney Creek Wilderness and Hercules Glades Wilderness. If you're determined to see indigenous wildlife, this is the place to go. For local flora, hit the trails at the **Henning Conservation Area** (334-3324), on West 76 just outside the Branson city limits, where free nature hikes are offered by the Missouri Department of Conservation several days a week from May through October. Each day highlights a different theme, from wildflowers to birds. The **Busiek Wildlife Area**, 15 miles north of the city, is a popular hiking spot. **Scenic Trails Vacations** (800-322-5048) in Ada can organize guided outings for you whether you want to bike or hike.

BOOKED FOR TRAVEL

Tomorrow on Rocky Pond, by Lynn Reiser, is a sweet book, delightfully illustrated, about an idyllic family fishing trip. Big kids can read this book to little ones and all will love the lists of paraphernalia, yummy meals and animal encounters. They'll also learn how to fish. (Greenwillow)

BEST BEDS: Every type of lodging imaginable has found its place in Branson. There are even full-outfitted houseboats available for rent from Houseboat Holidays (335-3042) and Table Rock Lake Houseboat Vacation Rentals (779-5214). For information on camping, contact the Missouri Campground Owners Association at 314-564-7993. Many of the campgrounds in the area rent cabins in addition to tent and RV sites. Some, like the Silver Dollar City Campground, feature playgrounds, recreation centers, a grocery store, laundry facilities, swimming pools and other family-friendly amenities.

Big Cedar Lodge (335-2777) is an upscale resort with all the trappings, including a *Kids Club* which runs three days a week in season. The Tribesman Resort of Table Rock Lake is a long time family favorite featuring lakeside cabins and homes. The resort has recently added a full-time recreation director and an indoor swimming pool in its efforts to please guests on a year-round basis. In addition to a variety of children's activities and a toddler toy/play room, owner Arno II regales guests with tales of the Ozarks.

Other useful services include Branson Vacation Reservations (800-221-5692), Ozark Mountain Country B&B (800-695-1546) and Ozark Ticket and Travel Network (800-233-7469).

WISCONSIN: WISCONSIN DELLS
Wisconsin Dells Visitors & Convention Bureau
701 Superior Street
Wisconsin Dells, WI 53965-0390
Information: 800-22-DELLS/608-254-4636

Unless otherwise stated, the area code is 608.

PROFILE: For families in the midwest, the Wisconsin Dells is synonymous with fun, a seemingly unending array of water and amusement parks, themed hotels, water sports and kid-friendly museums, plus 24-hour gambling at the Ho-Chuck Casino & Bingo.

Located in Central Wisconsin, the name Dells comes from the French word for gorge, *dalles.* Today, the fantastic rock formations that evolved during the Cambrian Period are as awe-inspiring as they were 150 years ago when the first written mention of the 18.2 square mile area appeared in the report of an Indian agent.

PLACES: Your first outing should be to explore the Dells, divided into the Upper Dells and Lower Dells, that guard the banks of the Wisconsin River, which can only be done by water. Various tours (**Dells Boat Tours:** 254-8555) visit the 15 miles of protected riverfront and sandstone cliffs from the middle of April to the end of October. The Upper Dells tour takes about two hours and includes disembarking from the boat for a short walk through a hemlock forest and passing though intricate sandstone gorges. The Lower Dells is about a one-hour non-stop trip. You can purchase the trips individually or in combination. Kids are certain to get a thrill as they splash along on a Lower Dells trip on one of the **Original Wisconsin Ducks** (254-8751), refurbished amphibious craft used during World War II for beach invasions. During the hour-long journey, the Duck plunges in and out of the water along the shoreline wilderness, up out of the Wisconsin River and over a sandbar into Lake Delton.

For an aerial view of the Dells, helicopter rides are offered by **Badger Helicopters** (254-4880) and **J.B. Helicopters** (254-6381) for as little as $10 per person. **Elusive Dream Balloons** (586-5737) will appeal to those who long to float aloft in peace and quiet.

Kids of all ages will enjoy the 28-acre **Wisconsin Deer Park** (253-2041) where, in addition to more than 100 tame deer, you'll spot elk, buffalo and many varieties of game birds. Animal lovers will be glad to know that there's also a petting and feeding area for close encounters.

Check out **Wonder Spot** (254-4224), one of nature's greatest mysteries. The site defies gravity, and everything seem a little off kilter. Things roll uphill; it's even difficult to sit down!

There are three daily tours at the **International Crane Foundation** (356-9462), where more varieties of crane are represented than anywhere else in the world. There's a chick hatchery, three miles of visitor trails and acres of prairie, marshlands, oak and cherry orchards, all restored to resemble the land as it appeared before the settlers arrived.

Hop into a horse-drawn carriage for a half-hour tour of **Lost Canyon** (253-2781). There are parts of these mile-long gorges that haven't seen the sunlight in over 50,000 years.

Fishing in trout ponds (pay by the inch for what you catch), and horseback riding (young kids can saddle up with parents) through a wildlife preserve and wild meadows with fox, pheasant and beaver are the top attractions at **Beaver Spring Preserve and Fishing Park** (254-2735). There's more fishing at **B&H Trout Farm** (254-7280), while riding is offered at **The Ranch Riding Stable** (254-3935), **Canyon Creek Riding Stable** (253-6942) and the **OK Corral** (254-2811). At **Wisconsin Dells Trout Farm and Canoe Trips**, guided fishing expeditions take you along the river to uncharted territory that's inaccessible to larger boats. Canoe rentals, tube trips and rowboats are also available at **Point Bluff Resort** (253-6181).

Two state parks — **Mirror Lake** (254-2333) and **Rock Arbor** (254-8001) — have hiking along nature trails and equipment rentals for biking and canoeing.

BEST BEDS: Though we haven't yet had the pleasure of visiting the Wisconsin Dells, friends from both Minneapolis and Chicago have been singing its praises for many years. Almost half of The Wisconsin Dells Travel & Attraction Guide is devoted to accommodations, listing resorts, motels, cabins, bed and breakfast inns and campgrounds.

Our friends' favorite places to stay include the Chula Vista Resort and the Holiday Inn Aqua Dome, both of which run children's programs in season. Kids' activities are also offered at the Yogi Bear Jellystone Park campground. A surprising number of hotels offer themed features such as "Polar Island" and "Glacier Mountain" water-park highlights at the Wintergreen Resort. "Lollipop Lagoon" is the new outdoor water activity center at the Carousel Inn and Suites with sections for toddlers and teens. The Wilderness Resort — An Adventure Resort features an indoor inter-active water area and the pirate-themed Treasure Island Resort, Hotel & Suites has an indoor wave pool among its attractions. The Polynesian Suite Hotel has two indoor water centers, one of which has a 40-foot pirate ship equipped with slides and cannons plus hand-activated geysers and a special area for younger children.

A number of more traditional condominium properties are available and many of the campgrounds also rent cabins. Small bed and breakfasts are yet another possibility.

BOOKED FOR TRAVEL

For children over 7, *The Kids' Book of Fishing*, by Michael J.Rosen, accompanied by **The Kids' Tackle Kit**, presents an in-depth introduction to the sport and provides everything but the pole, the bait and, of course, the place. To be honest, this looks like a pretty good book for adults too. (Workman)

My Nature Craft Book, by Cheryl Owen, has 42 imaginative projects for children. Most of them are simple enough to be done without adult supervision (obviously depending on age) and, many can be achieved using materials readily available at home. Though the majority of the projects seem to have a definite feminine slant, a number of them will appeal to both sexes. The illustrated directions are easy to follow, and the results should prove gratifying to the young craftsperson. (Little Brown)

WYOMING: JACKSON HOLE
Jackson Hole Chamber of Commerce
P.O. Box E
Jackson, WY 83001
Information: 307-733-3316

Unless otherwise stated, the area code is 307.

PROFILE: It's nature, nature everywhere in this land of wide open spaces. From the moment you arrive in Jackson Hole, the excitement of seeing its wonderful wildlife and glorious scenery keeps on building. Your first sighting might be a moose walking on the outskirts of town, the next a glimpse of pronghorn antelope up on the hills before you realize you're being distracted by the magnificent views of the surrounding Teton Mountains.

Whether you head for Jackson in summer, when more than 700 species of plants and flowers burst into explosive color, or come in the winter months when thousands of elk convene at the National Elk Refuge, the wonders of nature pervade.

Bounded on three sides by Bridger Teton National Forest, Jackson Hole is within easy striking distance of both Grand Teton and Yellowstone National Parks. Your biggest decision will be just how to do and see it all. Be guided by our suggestions, but don't be afraid to rely on your own spirit of enterprise. Don't forget to pick up a copy of *The Kids Guide to Jackson Hole* for your children. This 16-page booklet was written by a group of the town's 7th graders.

PLACES: Begin your adventures right in town, under the antler gates in the **Town Square Park**. In May, the annual *Elk Antler Auction* of the 9,000 pounds of antlers shed by the herds that winter on the **National Elk Refuge** (733-9212) is held here. The refuge is a five-minute drive down the road and an absolute must-see in winter. We were pleasantly surprised at how much we all enjoyed our visit to the **National Museum of Wildlife Art** (733-5771), which overlooks the refuge, and found the short film explaining its genesis particularly informative and engaging.

It was too late in the season to take a sleigh ride into the refuge, but we took full advantage of the telescopes at the museum. The museum galleries always have items of interest, the *John Clymer Studio* and the *Rungius Gallery*, after the *Children's Gallery*, were our boys' favorites among the permanent installations. We feel that the building alone, a massive stone structure that blends so well with its environment, is worth the visit.

In summer, head to the top of the mountain by taking the aerial tram at **Jackson Hole Ski Resort** (733-2292), where guided nature hikes are also offered, or board the chairlift at **Snow King Mountain** (733-5200) and, in summer, take the *Alpine Slide* down.

Getting into the wilderness is not difficult. We can't say enough good things about the **Great Plains Wildlife Institute** (733-2623), whose goal, according to Director and wildlife biologist Tom Segerstrom, is "to create unique wildlife experiences through participation, education and stewardship." We took a full-day expedition in a "safari" vehicle, with roof openings which allow for optimum viewing. Each participant is given binoculars as well as a field scope for even greater magnification. Our lesson in wildlife spotting began right outside of town. We learned where to look, how to identify what we saw and why the animals had migrated to a given location. Moose, elk, bighorn sheep, pronghorn antelope, trumpeter swans, nesting eagles, mule deer and coyotes were all in evidence. Sightings are recorded by the passenger in the front seat, a position that changes several times during the day, so that by day's end everyone has helped document the excursion. After a spectacular lunch at Gros Ventre River Ranch, we set off on snowshoes to track a recently-banded porcupine. Half-day, and even six-day expeditions are also offered, both in summer and winter, and they're worth every penny.

The **Yellowstone Institute** (344-2294) courses and outings for families have included *Nature Detective Workshops* aimed at specific age groups. Both the **Teton Science School** (733-4765) and the **Snake River Institute** (733-2214) also occasionally offer family classes. If your travels take you to the nearby town Dubois, stop in at the **National Bighorn Sheep Interpretive Center** (455-3429). A wonderful place for families to explore, there are interesting hands-on displays on the heartbeat and eyesight of sheep (which is seven times better than that of humans). The Center tends to the largest bighorn sheep herd in the world. There's an excellent walking trail and a wildlife viewing area as well.

A Personal Guide Service (733-1252) can arrange for just about anything in the vicinity, with "personal attention for older active people and families." Tours West (734-8311) uses custom vans for its winter and summer forays while Wild West Jeep Tours (733-9036) schedules three daily outings in spring and summer. Take your own car and hire Teton Jack Langon (733-4553), the "Old Man of Wyoming" as your guide. Having explored the area for more than 60 years, he claims to be the "single most experienced guide in the entire region."

Bring home incredible photographic memories after taking a day trip with noted landscape photographer D.J. Basset of Firehole Photographic Expeditions (733-5733). Explore the area with Wilderness Exposure (733-1026), escorted by Greg Winston who offers drives, hikes or canoe trips through "the heart of the Greater Yellowstone Ecosystem."

Scenic float trips (or challenging whitewater) on the Snake River are offered by Barker-Ewing (733-1000), Snake River Park Whitewater (733-7078) and Lone Eagle Whitewater (733-1090). Instruction and tours for families can be found at the Snake River Kayak & Canoe School (733-3127). O.A.R.S. (800-346-6277) offers two- and three-day kayak tours on Jackson Lake, including camping on Grassy Island in Grand Teton National Park and scenic float trips on the Snake River.

Hike uphill with a llama to carry your gear. Jackson Hole Llamas (800-709-1617/733-1617) will customize a trip for your family, while Black Diamond Llama (800-470-2877/733-2877) and Rendezvous Llamas (739-1639) offer one-day and multi-day trips.

Winter adds yet another dimension to nature excursions in Jackson. There are many reliable snowmobile and snowcoach tours into Yellowstone, as well as cross-country skiing and back-country tour operators in town. We set out early one windy, snowy morning for

Jackson Hole Iditarod Dog Sled Tours (733-7388). Run by Frank Teasley, a six-time Iditarod veteran, we were joined by a multi-genera-tional group that included an 18-month-old, a 4-year-old and their parents and grandparents. We were thrilled to be able to run our own sled and, boy, was it ever exciting! We admit, we fell off once, but we were never in any danger even though it seemed as if the dogs were moving very quickly. Teasley's full-day trip headed for **Granite Hot Springs**, where participants swam in the natural hot pool. Both before and after our trip we spent time watching Frank and his staff play with the dogs. It was a great day (except for the rank odors from the animals' food supply) and we got a sense of why being out in the winter wilderness for long periods of time can be appealing.

BEST BEDS: A wide range of accommodations are offered in Jackson Hole. It is important that you select the type of lodging that will best suit the type of experience you are seeking.

For example, if you're looking for a taste of the wild west, think about spending time at a guest ranch. Bear in mind that many of these ranches are all-inclusive and if you plan on taking daily excursions out into the wilderness, you may be paying for activities and meals that you might not take full advantage of. Therefore, if you plan on taking off on your own each day, opt for a facility where you are paying simply for your room, suite, cabin or the like.

Should your plans include skiing, you will most likely want to be close to the ski area since getting your kids to the ski school or nursery will be much easier. The Chamber of Commerce provides a listing of accommodations as does the Jackson Hole Central Reservations (800-443-6931).

In the ranch category Lost Creek, Heart 6 and Moose Head are all popular with families. Lone Eagle Resort and Dornan's Spur Ranch Log Cabins both offer a warm welcome to children. If you want to explore the wilderness by day and the town of Jackson by night staying at Snow King Resort is a good option. For skiing at Jackson Hole Ski Area, there are hotels and condominiums located right in Teton Village. The Alpenhof is the most luxurious, The Sojourner the largest and the moderately-price Inn at Jackson Hole features rooms with lofts that work well for families. Spring Creek Resort is a charming, rustic yet elegant full-service resort offering many amenities.

BOOKED FOR TRAVEL

John Hedgecoe's **Landscape Photography:** *A Complete Guide to Creative Ideas and Techniques*, makes professional techniques accessible to amateurs. Learn to take better vacation snaps or perfect your standards to an artistic level. Teenagers with a bent for the photographic will find this book as engrossing as an adult. (Sterling)

EAST

FLORIDA: SANIBEL & CAPTIVA ISLANDS
Sanibel-Captiva Islands Chamber of Commerce
P.O. Box 166
Sanibel Island, FL 33957
Information: 941-472-1080
　　or
Lee County Visitor and Convention Bureau
Information: 800-LEE-ISLE

Unless otherwise stated, the area code is 941.

PROFILE: Though Sanibel and Captiva are small in size, these two barrier islands off the coast of Florida in the Gulf of Mexico offer a wealth of opportunities for eco-travelers. More than two thirds of the islands' acreage is preserved as wildlife sanctuary and the beaches are a natural repository of more than 250 different kinds of shells. They were also the first islands ever to protect all of their wildlife, so it's no wonder that the International Osprey Foundation, the Marine Habitat Foundation and the Caretta Research Foundation (which works to protect the endangered loggerhead turtle) are all based here.

Unusual flora, from Australian Pine and wild jungle growth to the Gumbo Limbo Tree and the "official" joewood tree, and abundant fauna, from alligators and armadillos to manatees and pelicans, all flourish in this environment where nature rules.

Both islands can easily be explored by foot, car, bike, canoe, kayak, motor boat or trolley. There are more than 30 miles of bicycle paths, and fishing, sailing and windsurfing are among the other recreational activities.

PLACES: Named after Jay Norwood Darling, a pioneer of the American conservation movement, the 5,600-acre **J.N. "Ding" Darling National Wildlife Refuge** (472-1100) is Sanibel's ecological showcase and a sure-fire kid-pleaser. Among the year-round residents are osprey, nocturnal raccoons, large brown pelicans and alligators (most easily spotted during the spring and summer breeding seasons). At various times of the year, migrating songbirds, roseate spoonbills, yellow-crowned night herons and baby mottled ducks can be observed. Take the five-mile wildlife drive, hop on the tram, climb the observation tower, head for one of the three hiking trails or two canoe trails or take off on your bike. Fishing (but absolutely no shelling) is permitted in specific locations. The Refuge's Visitor's Center has lots of information and sponsors a variety of interpretive programs, including a 15 minute video overview of the refuge. Try your luck fishing in the back bay waters of the refuge with **Tarpon Bay Recreation** (472-8900) or take its guided canoe or kayak trips. There is also a clearly marked canoe trail you can take on your own.

The **Sanibel-Captiva Conservation Foundation** (472-2329) maintains the land along the Sanibel River, one of the few freshwater rivers still surviving on a barrier island. Nature trails, interpretive tours, a live marine touch tank in its visitor's center and an observation tower are all accessible to the public, as are field trips to local beaches and nearby undeveloped islands.

Your kids won't want to miss seeing the rescued animals at **CROW, Care & Rehabilitation of Wildlife** (472-3644). It's located across from the Recreation Complex at the Sanibel Elementary School, which has a fun playground plus tennis and basketball courts available for use. Tours of the facility are usually offered at 11 a.m. on weekdays and 1 p.m. on Sundays.

Before hitting the beach in search of shells, do a little preparatory homework at the **Bailey Matthews Shell Museum** (395-2233), the nation's only museum devoted to mollusca, with a collection of over 250 types of shells.

We were disappointed to learn that marine biologist Carl Melamet has closed his **Aqua Trek Center** (472-8680) and discontinued his hands-on *Sealife Encounter* sessions which we took years ago, when the "center" was in his garage. His ability to relate to and motivate even the most apparently disaffected kids was what struck us most. However, Carl is still operating summer programs for local youngsters that have accepted tourist children as well. **Adventures in Paradise** (472-8443), arranges a number of interesting outings: *History, Wetlands, Shores & Sea, and Interior Wetlands,* plus backwater fishing trips. Complimentary transportation is provided.

Canoe Adventures (472-5218) offers three trips that welcome kids. One heads for the Wildlife Refuge, another to the Sanibel River and the third to Buck Key. Most memorable for us was a guided birding excursion, canoeing through the mangrove at sunset with local expert, Mark "Bird" Westall.

The specialty of **Mike Fuery's Tours** (472-1015) are shelling charters that head to North Captiva or Cayo Costa Islands while **Wildside Adventures** (395-2925) at McCarthy's Marina on Captiva offers guided canoe, hiking and kayak trips and rentals.

Former zoo director John Heidger started **Everglades Day Safaris** (472-1559) in order to share the Everglades' beauty with tourists. In groups no larger than 10, visit a mangrove coast, sawgrass prairies, cypress swamps and Florida savannahs and finally land to take a nature walk at Big Cypress Preserve.

Run by the naturalist and shell expert at Captiva's South Seas Plantation **Shell Seekers** (472-5111) can take you on a three-hour excursion to the out island of Cayo Costa, north of Captiva. We loved the shell class we took when we stayed at South Seas. We learned more about shells and the islands than any of the guidebooks told us. Our son headed for the teen log-rolling event, after which we headed to the beach in search of bivalves and univalves, feeling so much smarter than other shellers we came across. Another operator departing from the South Seas Marina is **Captiva Cruises** (472-5300). On its morning *Nature Cruise* or late afternoon narrated *Wildlife Natural History Cruise* aboard the *Lady Chadwick* or the *Andy Rosse,* you have a good chance of spotting wild Atlantic bottle-nosed dolphin. **Club Nautico** (472-7540) puts you at the helm of your own powerboat to cruise, explore, waterski or fish.

BEST BEDS: The South Seas Resorts Company represents a number of properties on both Captiva and Sanibel.

South Seas Plantation is a large, sprawling resort on Captiva with clusters of "communities," offering more than 500 rental units. The one we stayed in was quite luxurious with magnificent views of the water and within easy walking distance to the main pools and restaurant. Even with the resort's complimentary transportation system, the location of some of the units will be best enjoyed if you have your own car. The resort has every imaginable recreational facility, including children's programs for ages 3 through teens.

We were quite taken by our visit to Sundial Beach Resort which is smaller and not quite as fancy. We especially liked the fact that all of the facilities were close to each other and that even the "fancy" restaurants had children's menus and the requisite high chairs. The kids' program is particularly focused on the environment (and was a big hit with all of our kids) and a bevy of family-together activities are featured each day.

The company also represents The Sanibel Inn, Song of the Sea, Sanibel's Seaside Inn and the Best Western Sanibel Island Beach Resort.

Other properties we know to be good choices are the 'Tween Waters Inn on Captiva (which also has activities for kids), Casa Ybel Resort and Sanibel Cottages on Sanibel.

Material sent by the Chamber of Commerce includes a complete lodging section.

BOOKED FOR TRAVEL

Unique Florida: *A Guide to the State's Quirks, Charisma and Character*, by Sarah Lovett, is guaranteed to raise everyone's spirits while on vacation. In this book you can find out about moonlight canoe trips, the Annual Manatee Springs Fall Festival (a Seminole Indian celebration), where to hunt for pirate treasure in the sand and, you guessed it, lots more. (John Muir)

NORTH CAROLINA: OUTER BANKS

Dare County Tourist Bureau
P.O. Box 399
Manteo, NC 27954
Information: 800-446-6262/919-473-2138

Unless otherwise stated, the area code is 919.

PROFILE: The Outer Banks of North Carolina, best known for the Wright Brothers' celebrated first flight, connote windswept beaches, sun-drenched sand dunes, salty marshes, wild horses and history. Scuba divers are irresistibly drawn to the many wrecks found in its waters, there's good fishing wherever you cast your line and each season new bike paths magically appear.

Formed by glaciers almost 20,000 years ago, these barrier islands are in a constant state of change. In spite of rapid commercial development, visitors can still escape from civilization on the wild and isolated beaches. When communing with nature has satisfied the soul, there is no lack of first-class accommodations and eclectic shops and restaurants; in short, this area has all the elements necessary for a relaxing and exciting family vacation experience.

We highly recommend that any visitor to these shores get a copy of *The Insiders' Guide to North Carolina's Outer Banks*. The authors, Mary Ellen Riddle and Thomas Yocum, obviously love their home, yet they don't hesitate to share both the positive and negative aspects of the area. They include all of the practical details on how to do just about anything that might tickle your fancy, offer up-to-date reviews of restaurants, lodging services and a chapter on *Kidstuff*. (The most important advice in the book is the need for insect repellent at just about any time, in any place.) If your bookstore can't get you a copy, order directly by calling 800-765-BOOK.

PLACES: Regardless of the island you choose for your temporary home, you'll find worthy natural adventures only a short drive away. Beginning in the north on **Corolla,** the 5,000-acre **Pine Island Audubon Sanctuary** is home to ducks, geese, sanderlings and other birds as well as deer, rabbits and foxes. Amid the oak, bayberry, ink -berry, pine, yaupon, and holly trees grow myriad varieties of sea grass. This wetland habitat is a major nesting area and open for tours to members of the National Audubon Society (see page 36) but is accessible to the public via a trail across from the Sanderling Inn or by car. Unfortunately, the advent of so many cars has obliged authorities to fence **Corolla's Wild Horses** into the 1,800-acre **Currituck National Wildlife Refuge.** Experts anticipate that it's likely the horses will manage to leave and return to Corolla in spite of efforts to keep them safe.

For breathtaking views and a glimpse of remnants of old shipwrecks, take a half-hour flight over the Outer Banks with **Kitty Hawk Aero Tours** (441-4460) on **Kill Devil Hills,** located near the **Wright Brothers National Memorial.** On **Colington Island** (part of Bodie Island) glimpse the inner workings of the commercial fishing industry. Set amid marshlands and forests, this is also a good spot to try your luck at crabbing. Don't miss the **Nags Head Woods Ecological Preserve** (441-4381), run by the Nature Conservancy (see page 40) in an effort to preserve the barrier island ecosystem. Departing from the Exhibit Center, there are tours, four-and-a-half miles of trails through forest, swamp, ponds and dunes, plus canoe and kayak trips. Among the summer adventures are bike-hikes, geology hikes, early morning bird walks and nature fun for parents and their pre-schoolers.

Further south in **Nags Head** you can see both ocean and sound from the top of a mile-long dune, 400 feet above sea level at its apex, in **Jockey's Ridge State Park** (441-7132). This area of shifting ridges is popular both because of its unique ecosystem and for its kite flying conditions. Natural history programs are sponsored by the park and a self-guided one-and-a-half mile nature trail identifies a number of plants such as persimmon and black cherry as well as tracks of raccoon, deer and hognosed snakes.

Down the coast a bit is **Roanoke Island,** where the *Lost Colony* settlers are memorialized both at the **Elizabethan Gardens** (473-3234) and in a performance at the adjacent fort. Visit working marine laboratories at the **North Carolina Aquarium** (473-3493) and inquire about the field trips, many of which are perfectly suitable for families. Be sure to bring your kids to the shark exhibit.

Hatteras Island's Pea Island National Wildlife Refuge (473-1131), where more than 265 species of birds have been identified, is probably the area's absolute must-see. In winter it's the nesting ground for swans, geese and ducks, while summer brings herons, egrets, avocets and black necked stilts. The Refuge offers a variety of nature trails and tours from its headquarters. **Hatteras Island** is also one of America's best windsurfing spots, a sport as colorful for the observer as the participant.

At the terminus of the Outer Banks, **Ocracoke Island** protects its wild ponies in the **Ocracoke Pony Pen.** The **Hammock Hills Nature Trail,** just three-quarter-mile in length, crosses the island from salt marsh through forest to the dunes.

For those who prefer joining an organized excursion, check out sea kayaking with **Outer Banks Outdoors** (441-4124) and **Shoreline Recreation** (441-1231), where you can rent ATVs, dune buggies, canoes and water scooters. On Hatteras Island, **Kitty Hawk Kites** (995-6060) sponsors daily workshops on sbjects ranging from kite flying to kayak nature trips. **Kitty Hawk Sports** (441-6800) in Nags Head, **Ride the Wind** (928-7451), **Ocracoke Outdoors** (928-4061) and **Wilderness Canoeing** (473-3270) in Manteo all offer similar fare.

A ream of family and children's activities are offered by the Rangers of the Cape Hatteras National Seashore, including a *Seashore Ranger* program for children ages 5 to 13. The outings take place at the **Hatteras Island Visitor Center** in Buxton, and information is available at the

Bodie, Hatteras or Ocracoke Island Visitor Centers. Each season the National Park Service publishes a newspaper, *In The Park,* outlining the various activities.

BEST BEDS: One week and longer rentals of cottages, condominiums and private homes appear to be the most popular choice of lodging on the Outer Banks. Consequently, there are an unusually high number of real estate companies that operate in the area, some which represent units in a particular area, others which represent the entire group of islands. The *Insider's Guide* provides a succinct round-up of these enterprises.

From all we've learned about the Outer Banks, the best way to select lodging is to first determine where on the islands you want to be situated. One of our newsletter readers is definitely biased toward the Corolla Light Community. The association offers events and activities, playgroups for children several days each week and many other family-oriented services. For information on rental companies, contact the Community Office 919-453-2455. Another reader swears that the only place to stay is at The Sanderling Inn Resort and Conference Center, located five miles north of Duck Village. This upscale resort has 28 rooms in its main building and 32 rooms in the North annex and features a wide range of recreation choices, including a fitness center and an indoor swimming pool.

Additionally, there are many motels and campgrounds from which to choose. When you request information from the Dade County Visitor's Bureau, they will send you the Vacation Guide in which a number of these options are featured.

BOOKED FOR TRAVEL

Magic Beach is a charming book with wonderful illustrations, each accompanied by a short verse. Author/illustrator, Alison Lester, has truly captured the essence of why a trip to the seaside is so magical for a child. (Little Brown)

VERMONT: WOODSTOCK & QUECHEE
Woodstock Area Chamber of Commerce
18 Central Street
Woodstock, VT 05901
Information: 802-457-3555
   or
Quechee Chamber of Commerce
Main Street
P.O. Box 106
Quechee, VT 05059
Information: 800-295-5451/802-295-7900

Unless otherwise stated, the area code is 802.

PROFILE: In the pastoral Connecticut River Valley lie the historic towns of Woodstock and Quechee. Though they differ substantially, together they offer visitors rich natural resources within easy reach.

Woodstock, often called the prettiest village in America (many of its buildings are listed on the National Register of Historic Places), has been a tourist destination since the late 1700s and enjoys a wealth of recreational assets. Three covered bridges, one dating to 1836, criss-cross this moated community.

Industrial Quechee was once a thriving woolen mill town. Today the main industry is tourism and the area is dominated by the planned development of the Quechee Lakes Corporation. The entire area is in close proximity to the Green Mountains and a hop, skip, and a jump from the White, Black and Ottauquechee Rivers.

It used to be said that Vermont had more cows than people but in their quiet New England way, the folks up there know quite a bit about being hospitable. Just think of all those feel-good Vermont associations: maple syrup, Ben & Jerry's, and Vermont Teddy Bears.

PLACES: A good place to start your visit is the **Vermont Institute of Natural Science** (VINS, 457-2779) in Woodstock. In addition to its rare herb exhibit, VINS boasts many species of flora and fauna, and the Pettingill Ornithological Library. Go on your own or join an interpretive walk along its nature trails, hike in hardwood forests and high meadows, watch beaver activity along the pond trail and don't miss the **Raptor Center**. This living museum is home to 25 species of birds of prey which cannot be released into to the wild due to their debilitating injuries. You can get up close to bald eagles and peregrine falcons, or drop in at the rehabilitation center for injured birds. The Visitor Center offers hands-on displays and seasonal programs that might feature anything from condors to wolves. Picnicking is welcome. Occasionally, VINS teams up with local lodging facilities, as it has with the luxurious **Woodstock Inn & Resort** (800-448-7900/457-1100). On a recent weekend, VINS guides set out with resort guests in search of varied thrush, frogs, whitetail deer, zebra swallowtail butterflies and other native wildlife.

Also in Woodstock, the **Billings Farm & Museum** (457-2355), named after a leading conservationist, is a working farm where dairying and maple sugaring (in season) are among the daily hands-on demonstrations. In its kitchen garden, learn about varieties of vegetables grown on the farms of yesteryear.

Head for **Faulkner Park** and take one of the walking paths around Mount Tom; rent a bike from **The Cyclery** (457-3553) and take off on the village bike path that crosses the Taftsville Covered Bridge; go for an hour-long or full-day horseback riding trip with **Kedron Valley Inn Stables** (457-1480) in South Woodstock. Demonstrations of maple sugaring also take place at **Sugarbush Farm** (800-281-1757), five miles from Woodstock. Though the sugaring itself is only done in mid- to late March, as a rule, the sugarhouse is open year round, as are the demonstrations of how cheese is stored and waxed. During the warmer months of the year, a baby calf at the dairy display is amenable to petting.

Ekiah Pickett's **Northern Pack & Paddle** (457-1409) is the place to turn to for a number of outdoor activities. Ekiah says he loves working with kids and families and thinks that too few realize how accessible the great outdoors is to them. He has spent the better part of his life exploring Vermont and its natural wonders and is eager to share his expertise. He puts it pretty well himself: "During the summer the forest screams with the sound of birds, animals and running rivers. During the winter it whispers with the sound of an owl taking flight, the light plop of accumulated snow falling from a pine bough and our own footsteps. Autumn is marked by Nature's own fireworks display." Whether you're looking for wildlife, scenic quiet water or a roaring river experience, Pickett's company can take you and your kids in a safe and fun manner. Ekiah also has a passion for fly-fishing and operates his own school. Among his other outings are canoeing, kayaking, hiking and winter snowshoeing with all the necessary equipment and instruction provided. Half-, full- and multi-day trips are scheduled.

A natural wonder, nicknamed Little Grand Canyon, **Quechee Gorge** located in **Quechee Gorge State Park** is an awesome sight. The best view is from above the Ottauquechee River in the **Quechee Gorge Recreation Area** (295-2990). A number of hiking and walking trails traverse the mile-long chasm. Biking, hiking, fishing, canoeing, and wildlife observation are the area's major activities plus the Woodsman's Museum and a narrow-gauge rail train ride. The entire region is considered ecologically sensitive and is listed on the Vermont Fragile Areas Registry.

While you're in the town of Quechee, stop at **Simon Pearce Glass** (295-2711) on Main Street and see how the dam's hydro power has been harnessed for the furnace where glass is hand-blown (and sold!). Rent a canoe, bike and learn to fly-fish or cross-country ski in winter with the helpful **Wilderness Trails** folks (295-7620) at the Quechee Inn who can arrange for equipment, lessons and guided outings, one of which heads for **Dewey's Mills Waterfowl Sanctuary.**

There's lots more a bit farther afield. Just a short ride down the road at Killington you'll find the **Merrell Hiking Center.** Hike the ski trails (or take the chairlift) for a view of five states from the top. Hike on your own or take the chairlift for a two-and-a-half hour guided interpretive hike where the "trails become your classroom to experience the outdoors first-hand." If you want to hike without your kids, check out **Killington's** *Alpine Adventure Day Camp* (422-6222) designed for children 3 to 12, that includes nature hikes, backpacking, swimming and fishing, and runs during July and August. A nursery for little ones (as young as 6 weeks) is also available.

Hook up with Tim Abraham of **Vermont Ecology Tours** (VET) (422-3500) for *Breakfast With The Birds of Killington*. You bring your own breakfast and Abraham supplies the rest—even child-sized binoculars. Red-tailed hawks, hummingbirds, warblers and woodpeckers will keep you company while you eat. Head for woodlands, lake shores fields and wetlands on VET's twice weekly *Nature Discovery Day* that follows the Robert Frost Interpretive Trail in the Green Mountain National Forest. Another of VET's specialties is a private tour of VINS and its Raptor Center. Abraham will be pleased to customize a tour for you. Tim is on the referral list of **Adventure Guides of Vermont** (800-425-TRIP), "a year-round stellar selection of guided outdoor services" that assists you in designing your own tour, whether it includes birding, nature hikes, hiking, wildlife photography, fly- and game-fishing, canoeing, kayaking and more.

Combine a healthy day in the outdoors with a stimulating museum visit at **The Montshire Museum of Science** (649-2200) in Norwich. Toddlers can explore safely in *Andy's Place* where there's a snugly bear den. The outdoor *Physics Playground* is designed to demonstrate basic scientific principles. Set in the middle of 100 wooded acres (particularly spectacular during fall foliage), cross-country ski trips and family nature hikes are often on the museum's schedule, depending on the season.

If the idea of hot air ballooning appeals to you, head for **Silver Maple Lodge** (800-666-1946/333-4326) in Fairlee. The 14-room B&B, located about a half hour from Quechee, is home to Scott and Sharon Wright and their young daughter. They can arrange hot-air balloon rides as well as inn-to-inn tours on bike, canoe or on foot.

There are several state parks in the area: **Silver Lake State Park** (234-9451), in Barnard (12 miles north of Woodstock), has a beach, playground, fishing boat rentals, youth programs and summer events such as music or story telling co-sponsored by the Vermont Council on the Arts; **Wilgus State Park** (674-5422) in Windsor along the banks of the Connecticut River offers fishing, canoeing and hiking on easy trails, including a short, relatively flat nature trails. In **Gifford Woods State Park** in Sherburne, the Appalachian Trail traverses the park. A stand of old trees there has been designated a National Natural Landmark.

The 40-minute **Green Mountain Flyer** (463-3069) train ride between Bellows Falls and Chester is a fun excursion about an hour's drive from Woodstock. If you head in that direction, visit the **Springfield Nature Trail**, which includes 55 acres developed by the Ascutney Mountain Audubon Society.

Other day trips include the **New England Maple Museum** in Pittsford or the restored 19th-century town of Grafton, where miles of woodland trails appeal to both walkers and bikers. Kids can see how cheese is made and stored at the **Grafton Village Cheese Company** or, if the time is right, watch a lamb being born at **Windham Foundation**'s sheep shearing facility (843-2211).

BOOKED FOR TRAVEL

Best Hikes with Children in Vermont is one of a series covering a number of states across the country. With any one of these in your backpack as your guide, you can head for the hills on excursions specifically geared to a child's age. (The Mountaineers)

BEST BEDS: When it comes to lodging in the Woodstock/Quechee Area there are two obvious choices: lodging at The Woodstock Inn & Resort, a grand elegant resort situated on the Green in Woodstock and renting from the Quechee Lakes Corporation.

Both are good choices but they are not the only alternatives. Both towns have motels (e.g. Shire Motel in Woodstock and Quality Inn in Quechee) and a number of country inns, farms and B&Bs welcome children.

Three Church Street in Woodstock Village is one B&B where children are often in residence. In addition to its 11 guest rooms, there's a swimming pool and a tennis court on the property. The Quechee Inn at Marshland Farm, built in 1783, has lots of outdoor (but little indoor) space for kids to run around in.

Within a half-hour radius the lodging choices widen considerably, extending to the Killington/Pico area where choices abound. The cottages at Silver Maple Lodge also sound appealing.

MEXICO

CANCUN
Cancun Tourist Information
P.O. Box 9018
East Setauket, NY 11733-3453
Information: 800-CANCUN-8

PROFILE: Cancun, Mexico's first planned tourist resort, offers a blend of Caribbean white sand beaches, modern hotels, shopping, dining and exciting nightlife. On two trips with our kids last year, we were quickly won over by its numerous charms. Expecting a strip of glitzy hotels that would sadly detract from the beaches, we were pleasantly surprised. The shopping, though more commercial than we generally enjoy, was particularly tempting for Americans (strangely, the shopkeepers wanted pesos, not dollars, in spite of the fact that the dollar rate grew stronger each day of our visit). Nicest of all, was that our kids bought presents for their friends without feeling pressed. The biggest surprise was the food, consistently good and fairly cheap. The kids loved Planet Hollywood; the Hard Rock Cafe had the best steak of our visit (and featured a room where we could listen to the music but also hear each other); and we joined those diners who went out and danced in the streets during our meal at Pericos, a repository of Mexican kitsch.

While we enjoyed the beach and the spectacular turquoise waters, we spent a good deal of our time along the Cancun-Tulum corridor in the province of Quinta Roo, where you're never far from a beach or a Mayan ruin. Though transportation is available to the places we highlight, we strongly recommend renting a car for a variety of reasons which will become clearer as you read on. Pack extra T-shirts for sun protection in your day bag. Many places (e.g., Xcaret and Xel Ha) don't allow the use of suntan lotion since it is not ecologically sound. We were all surprised to learn that outside of the hotels, used toilet paper is not flushed, but put in a bin, for the same ecological reasons.

PLACES: You don't even have to venture out of town to explore the natural environment. Right on the strip of hotels, you can head for the bottom of the sea. The kids in our small group, most of whom were too young to scuba dive, adored our ride on the **Atlantis Submarine** (children must be 4 and older) where we saw an unbelievable number of colorful tropical fish. Aboard **Nautibus** you can also get a view of the reef but the ship does not completely submerge. It is a perfect introductory experience to the world under the sea for anyone with the slightest feeling of claustrophobia as passengers can head up on deck at any time. Children under age 6 are free, ages 7 to 11 pay only 50 percent. Seasonal **Ecological Jeep Tours** are offered by Budget Rent A Car.

It takes a half hour by boat (public transportion is fastest and cheapest this time) to reach **Isla Mujeres**, yet it feels as if you're in another country; residents stroll barefoot and life in town in totally laid back, a far cry from the razzle dazzle of Cancun. Both neophyte snorkelers and daredevil divers should head for **El Garrafon National Park** a few miles outside of town. The park is five miles long and has great snorkeling (not always the case in Cancun, where surf can be rough). *The Cave of the Sleeping Sharks* is a major draw for divers. **Dolphin Discovery** (83-07-79) offers the opportunity to swim with the dolphins. Reservations are required and the minimum age is 8 with a parent, 12 without. Participants must be able to swim and the approximately one-hour session includes about 30 minutes of swim time plus photo opportunities.

From Isla Mujeres catch a boat to **Isla Contoy**, a bird lovers' paradise, about an hour's travel each way. This National Wildlife Preserve and bird sanctuary is home to flamingos, pelicans, cormorants, herons, magnificent frigate birds, spoonbills, pelicans and gulls and is an egg-laying site for endangered sea turtles. Almost one third of the world's known species of birds pass by this area. Great snorkeling is possible from the pristine, unshaded beach. Be certain to ask your guides if your tour provides lunch and what they serve (ours was grilled fish — great for the adults, but icky according to our kids who were starved) and if they carry child-sized snorkeling equipment (something else our boat didn't do). No food is available on the island. Be careful with whom you go. Avoid "party" boats as participants are encouraged to drink,

drink, drink all the way home — which they tend to do. Not exactly a wholesome family environment.

Driving down the coast, the first place of interest is **Crococun** (87-09-78), a massive reptile breeding station which is working hard to resurrect the almost extinct population of Yucatecan crocodiles. If it's warm, stop and snorkel along the beaches of Puerto Morelos, an area known for its great scuba diving. At the **Dr. Alfredo Barrera Marin Botanical Garden**, learn about the many uses of regional plant life, from coffee to mango. This 150-acre nature reserve offers hiking trails through a thick tropical forest and swamp where butterflies and orchids proliferate. However, during hot and humid weather mosquitos are also in abundance.

Less than an hour from Cancun is **Xcaret, Nature's Sacred Paradise** (98-83-06-54), an eco-archeological theme park that will be the highlight of your kids' stay. We've visited here twice, and each time wanted to go back for more. What's so enticing? Swimming with dolphins, horseback riding through the jungle, floating down the underground river, snorkeling in natural lagoons, seeing the tropical aquarium, the incredible sea turtle exhibit, the Wild Bird Breeding Aviary, the Botanical Gardens, the museum, the horses, the shows, the great gift shop, and so forth. You must be there when the park opens (unfortunately, the bus from Cancun does not get you there in time) to sign up for any of the hands-on dolphin experiences. A 4-year old was along when our kids spent almost an hour swimming with these incredible, gentle mammals. We saw one mom with an under-2-year old. Of all of the dolphin programs we've participated in, this was the best: informative, respectful of the dolphins and exhilarating for participants.

Once a bustling marketplace of the Mayans, as opposed to the royal city of Tulum, Xcaret's ancient ruins are interspersed among natural structures, such as the underground river and the amphitheater. Be sure to make time to see the rescued sea turtles (which are returned to their natural habitats as they get older), the eco-system display at the aquarium, and the fantastic bird and mammal exhibit. This well-managed park rents everything you'll need such as life vests, child-sized snorkels and masks. There are extra fees for masks and snorkels (except on the river float), horseback riding, dolphin programs and food, but everything else is included. Children ages 5 to 12 pay half-price, 4 and under are allowed in free. Try and plan your day with a map before you go (ask at the office in Cancun or at your hotel). We assure you that you won't be able to do it all in one day. We managed to see the horse show by lunching at the adjacent restaurant. Since our last visit Xcaret has grown (it's still only 50 percent developed). There are now two rivers to swim along only one of which remains underground; the Butterfly Garden is open (and best viewed in the morning); the park is now also open in the evening with an exciting array of shows and folkloric demonstrations called *Xcaret Nights*; the Mayan Village has been completed; a flamingo lagoon and a bat cave have opened. We can't wait to return!

Just south of here, at Puerto Aventuras, you'll find the free **CEDAM Underwater Archeology Museum. Indiana Jones Jungle Adventures** can take you to Nohoch Nah Chich, the world's longest underwater cave system (according to *The Guiness Book of World Records*).

Xel-Ha, eight miles south of Akumal, is one of the world's largest natural aquariums, with lagoons, coves and inlets offering some of the best snorkeling we've ever experienced—no waves, the clearest waters and countless tropical fish swimming amid a limestone seascape. There also cenotes (sinkholes, part of an underground water reservoir system), a partially submerged Mayan ruin and underwater caves. The range of equipment for children was impressive, with all sizes from the very tiniest. All equipment, including underwater cameras, can be rented, as can underwater cameras. Here, again, the restaurant was good with food the kids liked. Stop here after visiting the ancient city of Tulum which, though awe-inspiring, is also fatiguing, making Xel-Ha a refreshing and welcome respite. Now managed by the folks from Xcaret, a joint ticket for the two is certain to be in place soon. Some folks come for the entire day and there are lockers, showers, beach chairs, ample shade, lots of leisurely strolls, hammocks to plop into and kids everywhere. It takes about an hour and a half to return to Cancun.

It's well worth the almost two-hour trip to **Sian Ka'an Biosphere** (in Cancun, 84-95-83 or 87-30-80), a reserve with a mission to integrate the natural environment with the needs of the local community. Named a World Heritage Site in 1987, Sian Ka'an, which starts south of Tulum and runs all the way to the Belize border, is one of the world's most important coastal ecosystems consisting of tropical forest, wetlands and marine environments (including Gama Reef, part of the world's second largest coral reef). On our visit (which was enjoyed as much by the three teenagers with us as the 4- and 6-year- olds), swimming between our two small boats along an ancient Mayan canal in the Chunyaxche Lagoon was an awesome experience. We spotted a crocodile nest as well as osprey, herons, kingfishers and woodstorks. With our eyes in the sky we didn't notice many land animals but we hear that jaguar, ocelot and monkeys are often seen. This was the day we had our best lunch in Mexico, at **Cabanas Ana & Jose**, seven miles south of Tulum and very close to Sian Ka'an and from where tours into the Biosphere depart. The kids were in heaven when they discovered a trampoline on the beach and insisted on stopping there again before heading home.

On our next trip, we'll definitely visit **Coba**, 25 miles inland from Tulum. In addition to being one of the greatest archeological finds in recent years, it's one of the best birding areas in all of Mexico. Locals recommend showing respect for the site by asking permission prior to entering.

BEST BEDS: During our two recent visits to Cancun, we visited a number of hotels which welcomed families and offered a variety of organized activities for youngsters to enjoy. By and large, these activity programs were well-run and more than adequately staffed. Our only complaint is that almost all of them are run out of dark rooms located on lower basement level floors.

We spent a glorious six days at the Ritz-Carlton where the welcome for our kids matched the resorts' high level of service. On several occasions the younger children in our group asked to go back to the playroom (which was not in the basement but was far from a bright facility), always a good sign!

Unfortunately, the kids' program was not in operation when we stayed at the Caesar Park but subsequent reader reports have unanimously been positive. Almost at the end of the hotel zone, the Westin Regina offers a free kids' activity program plus a choice of both hotel rooms and apartment rentals. Marriott's Casa Magna has just put the final touches on its Club Amigos children's camp that is sponsored by The Cartoon Network.

Without a doubt, the most impressive facility for kids was at the Crown Princess Club, an all-inclusive resort with a water playground sure to please children of all ages. Kids' programs are also offered at the Camino Real (where a teen sports program is also featured), the Presidente InterContinental, Continental Villas Plaza, Hacienda del Mar and at several of the condominium complexes such as the Royal Caribbean. Some, but not all, of these are detailed in the *Cancun Vacation Planner* available by calling the telephone number listed above.

Rascals in Paradise (see page 74) offers a family package to Akumal year-round and also operates several *Family Weeks* there. You can also camp in style at Punta Bete (down the coast from Cancun) at Campout Kai Luum, where modern beachfront tents feature daily maid service and there is a choice of nearby restaurants. (800-538-6802)

BOOKED FOR TRAVEL

Let's Go Traveling in Mexico, by Robin Rector Krupp, is scholarly yet lively, an imaginary journey up and down and across Mexico, with Quetzalcoatl, the legendary plumed serpent, as personal tour guide. Whether your interest in Mexico is cultural, archaeological or ecological (or all three), this book will have both you and your kids raring to plunge into the Mexican experience and then go back for more. (Morrow)

Let's Go/Vamos: A Book in Two Languages/Un Libro en Dos Lenguas, by Rebecca Emberley, is a charming way to introduce children to the Spanish language. The collage illustrations are particularly appealing. (Little Brown)

CHAPTER 6

STAY & PLAY

Fortunately for many of us, environmentally-aware encounters do not automatically require moving around and packing and unpacking each and every day. This is especially good news for parents with babies and/or toddlers, who may not have the stamina for extended wilderness forays and for whom facing strange surroundings every day can be upsetting.

Almost all of the following resorts, inns or lodges feature some sort of children's activity program and offer private babysitters. As you'll see, our suggestions run the gamut from five-star resorts to cabins in the woods.

Serious "green" travelers might want to contact the **Green Hotels Association.** This organization encourages its member hoteliers to make their properties ecologically friendly. Their strategies include using nontoxic disinfectants in swimming pools, serving organic meals, recycling soap chips, using fluorescent lighting and asking guests if they are willing to forego daily laundry service and change towels and sheets less frequently. If you'd like to have a list of Green Hotels Association members, call them at 713-789-8889.

BOOKED FOR TRAVEL

If you prefer a smoke-free environment, look into **The Non- Smokers' Guide to Bed & Breakfasts**, by Julia M. Pitkin, in which you'll find descriptions of more than 2,800 such B&Bs in the U.S., Canada, Puerto Rico and the Virgin Islands. Most entries clearly state when children are welcome or list restrictions. (Rutledge Hill Press)

HYATT RESORTS

We begin with **Hyatt Resorts** (800-223-1234) — the first of the major hotel chains to commit itself wholeheartedly to servicing the needs and desires of the family market. It is still the only major hotel company to have a consistent, system-wide children's activity program, *Camp Hyatt,* which is viewed as dynamic and important so that Hyatt is always on the lookout for ways to improve and enhance it. The basic program is open to children ages 3 to 12, with kids divided into appropriate age groups. Though *Rock Hyatt,* a program for teenagers, has been discontinued at most properties, in its stead are a number of *Family Camp* activities, which we enthusiastically applaud. The goal of all these programs is to introduce the young and old alike to the natural environmental and cultural treasures of a given destination.

For example, at Beaver Creek in Colorado, kids hike the mountain to Beaver Creek Stables and families strap on snowshoes to learn about animal tracking in winter; in summer, they explore Bear Cave. In Puerto Rico, there's a family nature walk and snorkel tour; in Aruba, a kids' nature walk and a family glass-bottom boat cruise. Families learn how to husk a coconut or join a canoe race in Grand Cayman. Kids who love animals can study birds of prey in San Antonio and discuss endangered wildlife with the ranger at Kiluea National Wildlife Refuge on Kauai. The night sky takes center stage for families in Maui, while puppets act out the drama of the *Seasons of the Desert* in Scottsdale.

Our favorite Hyatt properties? Candidly, we've never visited a Hyatt Resort we didn't like (love, even). It's no accident that the Scottsdale's Camp Kachina was selected as the prototype for Camp Hyatt. The program was a huge success for years before Camp Hyatt originated. We'd return to Beaver Creek in a minute — it's a great hotel with incredible service, great skiing and terrific family fun. We can't remember ever feeling more pampered or welcome with our kids. Visitors on an Orlando theme-park vacation won't find more luxurious headquarters than the Hyatt Regency Grand Cypress. The sense of beauty and serenity of the properties in both Aruba and Kauai lasted long after our visits. The pools are reasons in themselves to visit either

Hyatt Regency Cerromar or Hyatt Hill Country San Antonio, both of which delighted the kid in all of us. It's not surprising that whenever we begin to discuss vacations, one of our kids' first questions is, "Can we stay at the Hyatt?" Both the *Camp Hyatt* and *Family Programs* are offered at the following properties. Most also offer enhanced activities at holiday times.

Property	Kids' Program Dates	Comments
Hyatt Regency Scottsdale, Scottsdale, AZ	Daily, year-round, 9 a.m.–5 p.m. Major holiday periods, 9 a.m.–9 p.m.	*Family Camp* offered major holidays and holiday weekends.
Hyatt Grand Champions, Indian Wells, CA	Daily, year-round 9 a.m.–4 p.m. Friday/Saturday, 6–10 p.m.	*Family Camp* not currently offered.
Hyatt Regency Beaver Creek, Beaver Creek, CO	Mid-December to mid-April, daily, 9 a.m.-10 p.m.; May through mid-December, Monday–Wednesday, 9 a.m.–4 p.m., Thursday–Sunday, 9 a.m.–10 p.m.	Camp not in session from mid-April until Memorial Day weekend. *Family Camp* offered daily, year-round.
Hyatt Regency Grand Cypress, Orlando, FL	Daily, Memorial to Labor Day, Week-ends remainder of year. 9 a.m.–4 p.m. and 6–10 p.m.	*Family Camp* offered daily, year-round.
Hyatt Regency Kauai, Kauai, HI	Daily, year-round, 9 a.m.–10 p.m. *Teen Rock Club* also offered Christmas, Easter and summer.	*Family Camp* offered Christmas and Easter holidays.
Hyatt Regency Maui, Kaanapali, HI	Daily, year-round, 9 a.m.–3 p.m.	*Family Camp* offered year-round
Hyatt Regency Hilton Head, Hilton Head Island, SC	Weekends, January to March, mid-April to Memorial Day and Labor Day through December. Daily, remainder of year, 9 a.m.–4 p.m. and 6–10 p.m.	*Family Camp* offered on a seasonal basis.
Hyatt Regency Hill Country, San Antonio, TX	Daily, year-round, 8 a.m.–10 p.m.	*Family Camp* is offered intermittently, generally on holiday weekends.
Hyatt Regency Lake Tahoe, Lake Tahoe, NV	Weekends and holidays year-round. Hours vary.	*Family Camp* offered weekends mid-June–mid-September.

Hyatt Regency Aruba, Aruba	All major holidays and summers plus weekends year-round. Friday evenings, Saturday/ Sunday, morning, afternoon and evening sessions	*Family Camp* only offered during "high demand" periods.
Hyatt Regency Grand Cayman, Grand Cayman, BWI	Daily 11/–8/31, 9 a.m.–4 p.m., 6–10 p.m. Weekends only remainder of year.	*Family Camp* offered daily, year-round.
Hyatt Regency Cerromar, Puerto Rico	Daily, year-round, 9 a.m.–4 p.m. and 6–10 p.m.	*Family Camp* offered daily, year-round.
Hyatt Regency St. John, St. John, USVI	Expected to be daily, year-round after reopening due to hurricane damage.	*Family Camp* offered Easter, Thanksgiving and Christmas only.

EAST

FLORIDA: Cheeca Lodge, Islamorada
Reservations/Information: 800-327-2888/305-664-4651

PROFILE: Few resorts maintain as strong a commitment to environmental responsibility as does Cheeca Lodge. Located in the Florida Keys, the resort understands the beneficial ramifications of protecting the area's natural resources. It not only maintains a nature trail that meanders along the length and breadth of the 27-acre oceanfront property, it also provides an informative booklet that urges guests to "get environmentally active" by outlining the many ecologically slanted programs on the property.

PROGRAMS: Fishing, diving, tennis and golf are among the many possible activities. The award-winning *Camp Cheeca* for children ages 6 to 12 says its "emphasis is on having fun and learning about the Keys' environment." *Camp Cheeca* offers full- and half-day programs year-round, operating from Friday afternoon to Sunday afternoon and on Tuesdays through Sundays during the summer and major holiday periods. On Thursday and Saturday nights *Kids Night Out* is offered.

PRICES: A mid-April to mid-December *Family Fun* package includes accommodations in a two-bedroom suite, unlimited tennis and golf, half-price *Camp Cheeca* and more for $285/night. A *Purple Isle Dive or Snorkel* package costs from $119 to $199/room/night depending upon the accommodation selected. In season, one-bedroom suites are $375, two bedrooms are $650; low-season prices drop to $285 and $495, respectively.

BOOKED FOR TRAVEL

The Green Guide, Florida: *A Travel Guide to Natural Wonders*, by native Floridians Marty Klinkenberg and Elizabeth Leach, visits state parks, forests, wildlife preserves and the like. A mix of personal experiences and down-to-earth how-and-when-to-visit facts, the book will suit both the dedicated eco-traveler or the tourist looking for a day out in nature. One could, for example, take time off from an Orlando theme park vacation and drive over to Lake Kissimmee State Park. There, visitors will find a reconstructed "Cow Camp" staffed by a ranger dressed and acting like a 19th century herder. The park also offers boating, camping and good opportunities for viewing wildlife. Other states covered in **The Green Guide** series are Hawaii and Vermont. (Country Roads)

GEORGIA: Little St. Simons Island
Reservations/Information: 912-638-7472

PROFILE: Located off the Georgia coast, Little St. Simons is a privately owned, 10,000-acre barrier island accommodating up to 24 guests in four lodges. This tiny resort has its own naturalist, six miles of unspoiled beach, fabulous food and comfortable accommodations. A visit to Little St. Simons offers the rare opportunity to explore a piece of the world that has been painstakingly preserved and kept glitz-free. There are no phones, TVs or air conditioners (rooms have ceiling fans). Guests reach the island via motor boat from St. Simons Island (a more developed neighbor), winding through a maze of tidal rivers and marshes.

PROGRAMS: The naturalist leads guests from the dock to the main lodge, passing under moss-bearded oaks, stately pines and graceful southern magnolia, identifying animals, birds and plants seen along the way. Jeep transportation to the beach two miles away is always available. There's plenty to do — shelling, horseback riding, surf fishing, canoeing, swimming in the artesian well-fed pool, crabbing, hiking, volleyball, bocce, photography, fishing, or hopping in a jeep in search of alligator nests or fallow deer. Most of the activities are led by the naturalist.

A *Summer Fun for Families* program, developed by a member of the naturalist staff, takes families to comb the beach, teaches about loggerhead sea turtles and spends an evening stargazing with parents and children. The program explains the surroundings in a way that both kids and adults can understand.

PRICES: Children must be at least 6 years old if visiting during high season, October to May; all ages are welcome during the summer. Low season rates begin at $290/night, at $375 in high season with children sharing with parents. In high season there is an additional $125/night charge for children. In low season, the charge is $75. Service (15 percent) and taxes (7 percent) are additional. Rooms accommodate a maximum of three people. Frequent kids free specials are offered during the summer. There are also rates for renting the entire island, something that is often done by large family groups.

MAINE: The Telemark Inn, Bethel
Reservations/Information: 207-836-2703

PROFILE: This cozy six-room Adirondack-style inn in the middle of the White Mountain National Forest, built at the turn of the century, is a "nature lover's paradise," according to owner Steve Crone. The Inn is bedecked with paneling and a large fireplace. Meals are taken around a huge dining table with a tree trunk base. Telemark Inn was the first place in New England to offer llama treks to the public.

PROGRAMS: There's eclectic and interesting outdoor fare to be found at Telemark year-round. When we first met Steve, he was leading a number of multi-day llama treks and canoe trips during the spring, summer and fall months. Sensing that families wanted a variety of experiences during their stay at the Inn, Steve designed a program that allows families to select from one-day llama hikes, canoe trips, mountain biking, horseback riding or a wildlife excursion, using the inn as a home base. Those interested in the multi-day trips can still opt for a three- or four-day trip or choose a combination three-day llama trek followed by a three-day canoe trip with a night in between at the Inn. We've spoken with many different families, including single-parent families, who all agree that Steve has a magical way with kids.

During the winter, sleigh rides, snowshoeing and cross-country skiing are featured. For kids, there are sledding, ice-skating, snowball fights, hikes in the snowy woods, marshmallow roasts and a chance to feed the inn's pet llamas, horses and goats. Although there's no formal kids' program, the Inn is a great place to take children with a "good time guaranteed for all!"

PRICES: Inn rates begin at $90/night based on double occupancy. A three-day all-inclusive package that covers meals, lodging and daily activities (see above) starts at $265/child 14 and under and $399/adult. Five-day packages are $425 and $595 respectively. Llama treks range from $75/adult, $50/child for one day to $525 and $375 for four days.

NEW YORK: Mohonk Mountain House, New Paltz
Reservations/Information: 800-772-6646/914-255-1000

PROFILE: Mohonk Mountain House was founded in 1869 by the Smileys, a Quaker family who wished to provide a wholesome country retreat for city dwellers. The Mohonk of the 1990s remains steadfastly rooted in its traditions. When you stay here, you'll be transported back in time to the days when people were accustomed to entertaining themselves and found satisfaction in a world without man-made attractions.

This 273-room "Victorian Castle," majestically situated on 2,200 acres overlooking Mohonk Lake, has 150 fireplaces, 200 balconies, gardens, picnic areas, a greenhouse, stables, a fitness center, a game room and 85 miles of hiking trails.

One way Mohonk expresses its commitment to the environment and ecology is with a dazzling array of themed weekends, from *Birding* and *Spring Nature* to *Summer Nature Week* and *Hudson Valley Harvest*. All programs explore the miles of surrounding nature and all it has to offer.

PROGRAMS: Needless to say, a resort with such creative programming looks after its younger guests imaginatively as well. Children's programs offer a wide range of activities, including boat rides, pony rides, rock scrambling and nature hikes. Campfires, hayrides, stargazing and night hikes are events the whole family can enjoy. *Tykes* (2 to 3) and *Children* (4 to 12) meet daily from mid-June to Labor Day, most weekends and holidays the rest of the year.

BOOKED FOR TRAVEL

Backyard Birds of Summer, by Carol Lerner, introduces young people to common North American birds they're likely to see in their yards or elsewhere in nature. The lifelike illustrations are sure to be an immense aid in identification. Although the book is full of information, the presentation is dry, making it more likely you'll turn to it as a reference. There is a second volume, **Backyard Birds of Winter**. (Morrow)

PRICES: As an example, nightly rates for weekend stays that include all meals and activities (except for horseback riding, massages and carriage rides) and children's programs range from $371 to $450 for two adults plus a $60 nightly fee for ages 4 to 12 and $90 for children over 12. Connecting rooms which share a bath begin at $469 for the first three guests with the same add-ons for children. Frequent mid-week specials are offered and there's a 10 percent discount on weekly stays. Several times during the year Mohonk *Family Weeks* feature free lodging for up to three kids under 12 sharing a room with their parents.

PENNSYLVANIA: Pocono Environmental Education Center (PEEC), Dingman's Ferry
Reservations/Information: 717-828-2319

PROFILE: PEEC is a private, not-for-profit center that was converted from a honeymoon resort to an outdoor "classroom." PEEC is located on 38 acres with access to over 250,000 acres of public lands. Ideally situated within the Delaware Water Gap National Recreation Area, it's the perfect place for an environmental center — the landscape is wonderfully varied with forests, fields, scrub oak barrens, ravines, lakes, streams, ponds, waterfalls and abundant birds and wildlife.

Guests are accommodated in 52 rustic cabins, which sleep from four to 12 people (one family per cabin) with single bunks and full bathrooms. We found the cabins more than adequate with the exception of the lighting. We brought a good flashlight for reading in bed on a subsequent visit.

PROGRAMS: Family Nature Weekends, held fourteen times a year, feature something-for-everyone activities for parents and kids to do together, e.g., canoeing with instruction, pond study, orienteering, birdwatching, making photograms in the darkroom and taking several hikes — one along a sensory trail, one with a guest naturalist-photographer and one at night. You can also participate in craft activities like candle-making or tie dying. There are evening square dances, campfires and lectures on topics such as *Birds of Prey,* to which the naturalist brings along an owl, a falcon and golden eagle.

The family weekends draw a diverse mix — babies through teens, single parents with kids and every possible ethnic background.

PRICES: Prices include lodging, meals and program activities. Guests may either bring or rent linens and blankets. Guests over age 4 pay $94 each for *Family Weekends,* $124/three-day *Holiday Family Weekends* and $164/*Weeklong Family Workshops.* Children 4 and under pay 50 percent; babies under one year are free.

VERMONT: The Tyler Place, Highgate Springs
Reservations/Information: 802-868-3301

PROFILE: This relatively small enclave on the shores of Lake Champlain, three miles south of the Canadian border, is run by three generations of the Tyler family and draws guests back year after year — our family among them. Each week up to 50 families, residing in either pleasantly decorated cottages, lodges or Inn rooms, are treated to three fabulous meals a day and a mind-boggling array of activities for all ages.

It's hard to describe the spirit of Tyler Place but it definitely evokes a sense of being in a large extended family. Everyone who comes is a parent (generally, but not exclusively, part of a traditional two-parent family). It's an eclectic group of folks, from stay-at-home moms to male and female lawyers, physicians, writers, professors, TV producers, social workers, teachers and others. Once you are able to secure a stay at Tyler Place, that week is yours indefinitely, until you give it up. Each year, as we make the five or so hour drive up to Vermont we wonder which families will be returning. When we changed weeks several years ago, our kids were initially disappointed not to be able to reunite with old friends. Fortunately, our "week" turned out to be frequented by another lively, interesting group of families whom we now look forward to meeting each June.

We put off visiting Tyler Place for several years because kids and parents did not take meals together. When this policy was changed to allow family breakfasts and lunches (even dinners in your cottage if you so desired), we quickly made reservations. You can only imagine our surprise when our boys chose to eat each and every meal with their peers! In spite of this, we found ourselves spending lots of time with the kids — even more than we do on most other vacations — and discovered that mealtimes were relaxing and — romantic.

PROGRAMS: In the mornings, kids and parents go their separate ways and meet up after lunch for "family time" when another wide choice of outings are presented. Your morning may include a canoe trip, a walk with local naturalist Doug Flock, or a hike with an ornithologist. Some folks opt for the mountain bike trips or hit the tennis courts. And, of course, there's the lake and all of the water activities associated with it. At dinner, the kids meet up again and stay together until their evening activity has ended. One of the newest niceties at Tyler Place, fondly called TP, is the booklet they give you upon arrival that describes numerous local excursions, the majority of which take you and your kids into the great outdoors.

The highlight at TP, however, is its extensive and excellent children's programs, eight in all: *Junior Midgets* (2 1/2 to 3), *Senior Midgets* (4 to 5), *Juniors* (6 to 7), *Pre-Teens* (8 to 10), *Junior Teens* (11 to 13) *Senior Teens* (14 to 16). Infants (newborns to 18-month-olds) and Toddlers (18 months to 2 1/2) are welcomed and are encouraged to come in the early (May-June) and late (September) season, when a morning playgroup is organized.

A parent's helper service (for a fee) provides one-on-one morning care, assistance at mealtimes and evening babysitting. It is always offered, so adults never have to miss out on the fun. Should your child get sick, TP supplies a babysitter at no charge to stay and play games with him or her for the same hours he or she would be in camp. All in all, TP is about as hassle-free as you can get.

When our older son Jordon turned 17 we almost gave up our week here, but we went at his insistence. Given the option of joining either the adults or the children, Jordon was in heaven, finding the best of both worlds. Now, at 18, he's still looking forward to returning, while our son Russell swears he will break all of the resort's records by returning year after year, even with his own children when he has them.

Activities take the kids the length and width of the 165 acres. The program coordinator has been working with a local naturalist for the past few years to expand upon the nature-oriented fare for children so that each day the group enjoys being outdoors while the kids learn about the local environment.

PRICES: Prices range from $110 to $174/night/adult. $45 to $64/ages 2 1/2 to 5, $48 to $68/6 to 10, $52 to $74/ages 11 to 16. Prices include all meals and most activities.

VERMONT: The Wildflower Inn, Lyndonville
Reservations/Information: 800-627-8310/802-626-8310

PROFILE; This charming inn boasts one of the most breathtaking panoramic views to be found in the state of Vermont, not to mention a heated pool (complete with waterfall and resident frogs), tennis courts and a baseball pitching machine.

To say that The Wildflower Inn is "family friendly" would be an understatement. The breakfast menu includes teddy bear pancakes complete with chocolate chips, while the converted barn is home to the Vermont Children's Theatre. Families wishing to dine early can place an order in the afternoon and a game room sits adjacent to the main dining room so that parents can relax and savor a meal, long after the kids have moved on to play bumper pool or dress up in the indoor playroom. Other delights include a barn with rabbits and ducks, swings, open fields, fishing, hiking trails, sleighrides and wagon rides — simple pleasures in a majestic setting with warm hosts.

PROGRAMS: In cooperation with *Vermont Worldwide Adventures,* the Inn offers a series of nature programs from June through September. The programs are recommended for ages 8 to 13, but younger ages are welcome with a parent or other adult. Some of the activities are: using plant fibers to make cordage, observing the community life of beavers at their pond, learning to recognize animal tracks on a woodland ramble and building a wilderness survival shelter.

Weekend wildlife programs for adults, such as *Coyotes, Cougars and Bears*, are scheduled from time to time and are taught by naturalists in an indoor/outdoor classroom setting. Daycare is available while parents are at their studies. On-site there are a petting barn, the Maple Sugar House, a tennis court, batting cage, soccer field and more. Off-property you might head to Willoughby Lake, a glacier-carved wonder, or try your luck at a local golf course.

PRICES: Rates, which include a full country breakfast and afternoon snack, depend on the type of room, ages of the children and time of year.

An average family of four with one child under 6 and the second between the ages of 6 and 8 would pay from $113 to $185/night and $635 to $1,035/week. Rooms with private baths have one double bed and bunk beds, a studio includes a kitchenette and the three-room family suite comes complete with two bedrooms, living area and kitchen. There are also rooms with shared baths.

BOOKED FOR TRAVEL

Quiet Water Canoe Guide, New Hampshire, Vermont: *Best Pad-dling Lakes and Ponds for All Ages,* by Alex Wilson, is one of those books whose title sums it up. You'll discover not only the best bodies of water for canoeing, but also where to camp, what wildlife you may spot, etc. (Appalachian Mountain Club)

In **Frogs, Toads, Lizards, and Salamanders** Nancy Winslow Parker and Joan Richards Wright have cleverly found a way to present their subject so that it will capture the interests of kids from preschool age through teens (not to mention adults). For example, on the left page you'll find, "Onto Patty's pie a la mode, Hopped a large American Toad," with a suitably humorous illustration. The right-hand page is scientific in its bent, with accurate drawings of *bufo americanus* and a short treatise on its living patterns carefully couched in language a child will comprehend. The last several pages delve deeper, into life cycles, anatomical cross sections, range maps, a glossary and scientific classification of these members of the classes *amphibia* and *reptilia.* It's a brilliant and enter-taining book. (Mulberry)

VIRGINIA: Wintergreen Resort, Wintergreen
Reservations/Information: 800-325-2200/804-325-2200

PROFILE: It's a hard call as to when nature is at her most glorious at Wintergreen Resort in Virginia's Blue Ridge Mountains. This is truly an all-season destination, with activities that include skiing, snowboard-ing, lake and pool swimming, golf, tennis, horseback riding, 30 miles of hiking trails and canoeing on Lake Monocan.

Dramatically placed atop the mountain range, the resort has villas, condominiums and homes that can accommodate anywhere from two to 14 guests. The only complaint we've ever heard about Wintergreen is that it is so spread out, families sometimes wish they had two cars at their disposal so it would be easier to get each family member to his/her desired activity.

PROGRAMS: Kids are always welcome at Wintergreen. There's an annual *Teen Outdoor Adventure Camp,* a three-and-a-half-day overnight wilderness trek with mountain biking, a rope course, and canoeing down the James River. Younger children who are ready to try overnight camping can enroll in one of the *Kid's Nature Camps*, where kids are divided by age and activities share a common theme. *Camp Wintergreen*, with events like salamander expeditions, butterfly walks and night hikes, is broken up into sessions for children 21/2 to 5 and 6 to 12. The whole family will enjoy the horseback riding, tennis clinics or golf. Special nature-oriented weekends are often on the agenda. One such weekend is the *Spring Wildflower Symposium,* another is *Fall Foliage in the Blue Ridge.*

PRICES: For a two-bedroom condominium you would pay from $200/night, $510/three nights and $1,078/seven nights in the value season, $250/night, $639/three nights and $1,351/seven nights in high season (summer and fall). A variety of ski and golf packages are offered.

BOOKED FOR TRAVEL

From New Jersey to Virginia, the **Seasonal Guide to The Natural Year: Mid-Atlantic**, by Scott Weidensaul, steers dedicated naturalists on the lookout for flora and fauna to the most likely spots to espy their quarry. From beaver dams to the breeding grounds of bugling elk, from whale watching to wildflower trails, this book tells you when, where and how. (Fulcrum)

CENTRAL/ROCKIES

COLORADO: The Nature Place, Colorado Outdoor Education Center, Florissant
Reservations/Information: 719-748-3475

PROFILE: In the shadow of Pike's Peak, near Colorado Springs, The Nature Place is so well regarded it has been designated a *Nature Environmental Study Area* by the National Park Service. It's no wonder that when the Smithsonian Institute experimented with family programs, it chose to head to The Nature Place, where "nature programs are for all ages to enjoy and include activities which investigate astronomy, geology, birds, wildflowers, photography, human history and more. Activities are designed so everyone can gain a better appreciation of our place in nature with fun and adventure emphasized." In summer, mountain biking, horseback riding, fishing and camping are possible while winter offers cross-country skiing, ice-skating and sledding in this wonderful wilderness refuge.

The modern studio apartments, constructed out of native rocks, wood and glass, each include kitchenette, fireplace, twin or double beds, and a loft with sleep sofas — like a home away from home. A recreation complex has an indoor pool, indoor sports court, jacuzzi, sauna and exercise room.

PROGRAMS: The Nature Place is open year-round. Special *Adventure Weeks for Families* are offered at various times and welcome all family members, from infants to grandparents. Each day guests head out onto the 6,000-acre property and beyond in search of wildflowers, birds, fossils and the like.

Though the majority of the activities are family-together events, kids-only favorites are offered each week and include hiking, animal tracking, learning about edible plants and more. When the activity is too strenuous for younger children, staff members stay behind to entertain them on-property. The Interbarn building, the center's focal point for educational displays, features a giant walk-in cell and a planetarium. It is always a big hit with kids.

PRICES: Nightly rates for a family of four begin at $105 for the first adult, $85 for the next (or a child 16 and over), $65 for a child age 5 to 15. Under 5 is free. The six-day programs are $690/anyone 16 or older, $500/children 5 to 15. All rates include three meals a day, use of facilities and educational programs.

COLORADO: Keystone Resort, Keystone
Reservations/Information: 800-222-0188/970-468-2316

PROFILE: Keystone has been catering to families since the day it opened; now it boasts nearly 100 activities for parents and kids. No matter what time of year you visit there's always plenty to do. Warm weather highlights include guided llama treks from the top of the mountain and nature walks through Arapaho National Forest with the best-of-all-possible guides — a U.S. Forest Service Ranger. Especially popular is a new 40-acre Wetlands Park along the Snake River. In addition to a number of interpretive exhibits, guests can observe the ecosystem from a boardwalk. There's also the option of traveling to Breckenridge to whoosh down its Alpine SuperSlide and then finding the path through the giant Amazin' Maze. Plus, there's mountain biking, river rafting, in-line skating, a full-service spa (for women only!) and skiing through the month of June. When the snows come, Keystone becomes a full-service ski resort with all the trappings: downhill skiing, snowshoe tours and cross-country excursions. Year-round, you can head to the Continental Divide.

For years we've believed that Keystone epitomizes the ideal vacation for an active family, especially for those who want to stay together but not always play together. The resort's internal transportation system allows family members easy access to all of its facilities. Our kids used it all by themselves when they were only 8 and 11 years old and we felt very comfortable giving them this freedom. The transportation department can even arrange to take you to the grocery store!

Another nice aspect of Keystone is its many lodging choices — from a great number of condominium clusters to comfortable rooms at the Inn at Keystone to luxurious accommodations at Keystone Lodge.

Eateries are conveniently located at the resort and range from family restaurants to gourmet fare.

Several of our winter vacations have taken us to Keystone and they have all been outstanding. We'll cover this area in greater depth in the ski chapter of **Great Sports Vacations With Your Kids.**

PROGRAMS: The year-round *Keystone Children's Center* welcomes ages 2 months to 12 years old with kids placed into age appropriate groups. In summer, *Keystone Nature Walks* are offered several times a week and include *Beaver Prowl, Wildflower Walk* and *Discover Keystone Valley.* These walks are most appropriate for children 8 and older. A list of Teen Activities can be found at the Recreation Desk in the resort. In winter, the program focuses on skiing on Keystone's three mountains.

PRICES: Prices vary season to season. Expect to pay from $110 to $175/night for a hotel room with two queen beds and from $180 to $290/night for a two bedroom/two bath condominium.

BOOKED FOR TRAVEL

"The outdoors is one giant, adventurous playground for children, full of fun and surprises around every corner." Positive and practical, Michael Hodgson's **Wilderness With Children:** *A Parent's Guide to Fun Family Outings* has chapters on camping, cross-country skiing, canoeing, kayaking and biking plus checklists, suppliers, first aid information — in short, just about everything you need to know before you head for an outdoors adventure with your children. Most chapters end with a list of *Tips in a Nutshell.* Hodgson is a father and not afraid to practice what he preaches. His daughter, Nikki, went on her first camping trip at the age of one month. A very down-to-earth, useful resource. (Stackpole)

MINNESOTA: Ludlow's Island Resort, Lake Vermilion
Reservations/Information: 800-537-5308/218-666-5407

PROFILE: Ludlow's Island Resort has just 18 cabins nestled among birches and pines on the shores of beautiful Lake Vermilion. The cabins range in size from one to five bedrooms and include fireplaces, full kitchens and outdoor decks. All cabins come with their own 16 foot motor boat and the off-island cottages have their own canoes as well. Pretty much anything you do on this northwoods island, whether on land or water, will bring you into contact with nature. An information book found in each cottage describes some of the wildlife you're apt to encounter: loons, bald eagles, bears, deer, moose and beavers.

PROGRAMS: Though there's no formally structured program for kids, all sorts of environmentally-themed activities are planned and held intermittently every week for the children who are on property that week. Children can plant tree seedlings and learn about reforestation, for example, or take a pontoon excursion out to a beaver lodge to look out for ducklings, loons or even a bald eagle. Native American crafts, cookouts and movies are also scheduled. Children love the tree house, water slide, roped-off swimming area along the sandy beachfront, the camping island and the game room. It's hard to decide whether it's the kids or the parents who best enjoy the big-wheel water tricycle!

Each day guests are greeted with a daily activity schedule listing a variety of both on- and off-property excursions. There are weekly fishing clinics, 365 islands in the lake to explore and a self-guided nature trail. Off-property, there are day hikes to Vermilion Falls and to Vermilion Gorge in Superior National Forest. Visit the International Wolf Center at Ely, the Cold Spring Deer Farm, take a bog walk or ride a miniature train through Tower Mine, 2,400 feet underground. If you time your visit right, you may get lucky and witness the Northern Lights.

PRICES: Ludlow's season runs from May to October and all stays are a week in length. Weekly rates for 1996 range from $1,175 to $1,850.

BOOKED FOR TRAVEL

Antler, Bear, Canoe: *A Northwood's Alphabet Year,* by Betsy Bowen, depicts the lure and the lore of Minnesota life in 26 charming vignettes. The colored woodblock prints are exceptional. This book will delight the youngest to the oldest reader. (Little Brown)

OHIO: Deer Creek Resort & Conference Center, Mt. Sterling
Reservations/Information: 800-AT-A-PARK/614-869-2020

PROFILE: Between Columbus and Cincinnati in the town of Mt. Sterling lies Deer Creek Resort, an Ohio State Park Resort with 110 luxurious rooms, including suites, lodges and 25 two-bedroom housekeeping cottages. There's no lack of recreational activities here — possibilities include golf, tennis, indoor and outdoor pools, a fitness room, boating, fishing, basketball, jogging trails, bike rentals, cross-country trails (in winter) and more.

PROGRAMS: Because the resort is located right in the park, there's a full range of nature programs literally at your doorstep; some are designed just for kids, but most the entire family can enjoy together. The Nature Center is open from 7 a.m. to 8 p.m. daily. Contact the Park Office at 614-869-3124 for a schedule of weekly events.

A wide and varied activity schedule, which runs intermittently day and evening, is offered for all ages. Twice weekly the *Doe & Buck Club* (ages 3 to 12) meets for dinner and an activity. Teen programs are also scheduled on those evenings. Currently the resort's naturalist program for kids has been put on hold as families tend to spend lots of time exploring together. The kids' activities run on the hour throughout the day. Ask about the park's *Naturalist Aide Program* for children ages 7 to 14.

PRICES: Nightly rates begin at $85/double room and soar as high as $600/large cottage.

WEST VIRGINIA: Oglebay Resort, Wheeling
Reservations/Information: 800-624-6988/800-633-9975-Canada/304-243-4090

PROFILE: Located in the hills of northern West Virginia, Oglebay Resort began life as the elegant summer estate of Colonel Earl Oglebay, an industrialist who willed the property to the citizens of Wheeling "for recreational and educational purposes." Oglebay continues to be a nature sanctuary featuring the excellent Good Children's Zoo, the Brooks Nature Center, a garden center, greenhouse, observatory and planetarium.

For recreation there are two golf courses, a par-3 course, indoor and outdoor tennis courts, indoor and outdoor swimming pools, fishing, two playgrounds and boating on Schenk Lake. There's even a miniature golf park at the Children's Center. In winter cross-country skiing and ice-skating are offered.

Accommodations include the choice of staying at one of more than 200 rooms at Wilson Lodge or at one of almost 50 cabins in the woods. Cabins are fully outfitted and have from two to six bedrooms, central heating, stone fireplaces and full kitchens. There are several restaurants on the grounds of the resort.

PROGRAMS: There are miles of wooded trails for hiking, an arboretum, guided nature walks, gardening courses, astronomy classes, fishing and paddleboating. For children, the specialized camps are among the most highly regarded in the nation. *Zoocamp* for children ages 4 to 9 (divided into ages 4 to 6 and 7 to 9) and *Nature Day Camps* for ages 7 to 10 run during the summer months. The *Nature Day Camps* are operated by the Oglebay Institute's A.B. Brooks Nature Center (304-242-6855). The resort's golf and tennis centers also offer clinics and workshops for children.

PRICES: During the summer, packages in standard rooms (maximum five people) begin at $130/night/Monday to Thursday, $150/Fridays and Saturdays and $110/Sundays, and include breakfast for two and a number of recreational activities. Without these features rates are $89/midweek and $109/weekends. Children always stay free and kids ages 6 and under eat free. Cottage rates range from $150 to $325/night in summer and from $590/week/off-season to $1,25/high-season. Cottages sleep from eight to 24 people.

WYOMING: Grand Targhee Ski And Summer Resort, Alta
Reservations/Information: 800-TARGHEE/307-353-2300

PROFILE: Located in the heart of Targhee National Forest, next to Grand Teton National Park, Grand Targhee boasts panoramic views across three states. And, regardless of which entrance route you choose, you're bound to see abundant wildlife in the surrounding mountains every step of the way.

In winter, one of the big draws is the snowcat skiing, which, our teens exclaimed, was the best day of skiing they'd ever experienced. Read more about this in **Great Adventure Vacations With Your Kids**.

We absolutely loved every moment of our visit to Grand Targhee. The skiing was superb, the ambience even better. Our evening hayride dinner, made and served in a yurt, was great fun and the views were utterly divine. En route to dinner we passed a family of deer in the woods and tried to identify several sets of animal tracks.

Guests have a choice of staying in one of the 32 condominium units or the 63 guest rooms at either of the two lodges, all located in the base village and convenient to all of the mountain activities, restaurants and shops. The resort's Climbing Wall welcomes adults and children ages 5 and older. A new spa has recently opened, something we always find a soothing delight after an active day outdoors.

PROGRAMS: Though it's best known to skiers who sing its praises, Targhee's summer offerings more than match its winter fare. Among the choices at this incredibly family-friendly resort are nature trails, hiking, visits to Yellowstone and Teton National Parks, horseback riding, rafting, mountain biking and much more.

As for the kids, *Baby Club* welcomes kids ages 2 months to 2 years and *Kids Club* is for children ages 3 to 10. Both require reservations and feature a number of nature-oriented activities. An annual summer highlight for kids is the *Science Explorers Day Camp* at the Targhee Institute for ages 8 to 12. Six hands-on programs are offered. Past classes have included: *Rock and Roll Geology; Nature's Kings: Predators Large and Small; Exploration Earth;* and *Growing and Gathering*

Snackables. Sessions run from Monday to Thursday and kids can participate for just one day if they like. Classes are, of course, also offered to adults.

PRICES: From June through August, lodge rooms range from $59 to $93/night, condominiums from $92 to $170. In winter, a three-night lodge stay costs anywhere from $175 to $330, condos from $285 to $400, seven nights from $360 to $700 in the lodges, $600 to $875 in the condos. Kids 14 and under stay free. Winter packages include adult lift tickets and cross-country trail access.

WEST

HAWAII: The Mauna Lani Bay Hotel & Bungalows, Kohala Coast
Reservations/Information: 800-367-2323/808-885-6622

PROFILE: On the Kohala Coast of the Big Island of Hawaii, the **Mauna Lani Bay** is a sleek and sophisticated resort, with teeming fishponds, perfectly landscaped gardens, terrific food, and a fabulous beach with hammocks, hooded cabana chairs, well-groomed sand and a lagoon situated on a particularly calm stretch of water replete with fish and turtles. In addition to the great beach are the royal fishponds of King Kamehameha himself, petroglyph fields, two championship golf courses, tennis, a spa and lots more.

Accommodations feature tones of white and beige accented by teakwood and all of the rooms have private lanais. Five private bungalows, each 4,000 square feet in size, are the epitome of luxury with steam baths, whirlpool spas and 24-hour butler service. One- to three-bedroom villas, ideal for families, have laundry facilities.

PROGRAMS: Located on the site of an ancient lava flow, the lush grounds are dotted with parks, preserves, caves and fishponds. Incredible sunsets, imposing volcanoes and an unmatched setting make a visit to the Mauna Lani Bay a special treat.

Eco-Teen Adventures is an innovative "green-minded" program for ages 13 to 17, that runs when teens are on the property (generally from mid-June through Labor Day and during major school holidays). The on-site (or just off-shore) activities include *Green Sea Turtle Rearing, Moonlight Reef Walking* and *Teen Tennis*. There is also a selection of expeditions — overnight sea kayaking, reef free-diving, wilderness hiking and a teen deep sea charter. The seasonal *Camp Mauna Lani Bay* for ages 5 to 12 has both day and evening programs and features nature walks, lei making, reef explorations and petroglyph rubbing.

PRICES: A *Family Suites* package that can accommodate six people includes two connecting rooms for the price of one, plus a children's mini-bar stocked with juices, a VCR, junior-sized bathrobes and a welcome basket of goodies. Cost is about $430/night. Parents can also share a room with their children and pay regular rates or pay full price for the first room and 50 percent for an adjoining room for the children. Special packages are almost always offered.

MONTANA: Lake Upsata Guest Ranch, Ovando
Reservations/Information: 800-594-7687/406-793-5890

PROFILE: On the shores of a spectacular mountain lake in the Black Foot Valley of western Montana, Lake Upsata Ranch promises guests "a truly unique recreational and educational experience . . . where people, young and old, can re-establish a bond with nature." You can lodge in a comfortable, rustic cabin, but your kids will love you forever if you go for the second option — a tipi. Packages can include three meals a day, horseback riding and instruction, fly-fishing with a guided half-day tour, wildlife programs and nature hikes.

PROGRAMS: Wildlife biologists lead a weekly program focusing on wolves, elk, water fowl, owls and the relationship of Native Americans with the animal kingdom. They also run a naturalist course. The objective is to offer just the right balance of recreation and education to ensure a great vacation for everyone.

Programs are for both adults and children. The children's version of the wildlife and nature program features swimming, boating, canoeing and kayaking, mountain biking, playing volleyball and horseshoes, making crafts (e.g., creating Indian folkloric dream catchers, pressing and laminating wildflowers) and fly-fishing. Kids might catch and view bugs through a microscope then head off for an afternoon of tubing or playing in the treehouse. Evening campfires and barbecues are part of the fun.

PRICES: Rates are about $195/adult/night, $165/child 12 and under. A three-night minimum is required. Kids 4 and under stay free. Tipis cost $100/person/night.

When you're outdoors, it's always fun and satisfying to be able to point out and recognize the members of the animal kingdom you encounter. **Common Campground Critters of the West:** *A Children's Guide,* by Jean Snyder Pollock and Robert Pollock, should inspire your kids to sit up and start looking around. The text, however, will most likely require the assistance of a parent. (Roberts Rinehart)

UTAH: Sundance Resort, Sundance
Reservations/Information: 800-892-1600/801-225-4107

PROFILE: The dream of Robert Redford, set amid mountain streams and thousands of acres of protected wilderness at the base of Mount Timpanogos, Sundance is "about the enjoyment of Nature's gifts of peaceful space, recreation, and food in a way that preserves the pristine character of the region." These noble ideals translate into a low-key, relaxed family vacation environment. Hiking trails, horseback riding, mountain biking and fly-fishing are among the most popular recreational activities.

PROGRAMS: According to one of our newsletter readers, "Sundance is a small, intimate 80-room development nestled into the hillside of a beautiful 6,000-acre canyon. The rooms are cabin-like and blend in with the surroundings. The staff is extremely friendly, helpful and courteous. The food is outstanding — an eclectic mix of Southwestern, traditional and contemporary American cuisine utilizing organic produce grown on Sundance's own farm. Sundance's pricing is comparable to those of other resorts of its quality. Though there is no pool, guests can use the facilities of a health club for a small fee.

"There's a lot to do at Sundance — horseback riding, mountain biking and hiking on property; golf and whitewater rafting can be arranged for nearby. Fly-fishing is also a specialty, thanks to *A River Runs Through It*. My wife and I, both inexperienced riders, went on two guided trail rides up into the mountains. Though we visited in the spring, winter is not without its sporting opportunities, including on-site downhill and cross-country skiing on groomed trails and snowshoeing. While all of these recreational activities can be found elsewhere, it is its theater, film and children's programs that make Sundance unique."

In summer, *Sundance Kids* for children 6 through 12 concentrates on nature study, Indian crafts and legends, hiking and riding. A schedule of three-day camps runs from mid-June through Labor day from 9 a.m. to 4 p.m. and is complimentary to resort guests. In winter Sundance offers a children's ski program, minimum age 4.

PRICES: High season is July and August and mid-December through March, when the average rate for a family of four is about $410 for a two-bedroom unit. In winter the rate includes two adult lift tickets per day plus admission to the film series. Kids stay free and ski free at that time as well. In low season, the rate drops to about $330.

BOOKED FOR TRAVEL

No question about it, if your travels take you to Washington, Oregon, Idaho and/or British Columbia, **Going Places:** *Family Getaways in the Pacific Northwest* is a book you'll want to consult frequently, both before and during your journey. Co-authors Ann Bergman and Rose Williamson are *the* family travel experts in the region. Bergman is founder of four parenting papers in Washington and Oregon. The book is well organized, full of right-on details on urban and rural lodging, eating and activities, and doesn't pull any punches. Interspersed throughout the book are parents' comments, some good, some bad. In addition to a complete alphabetical index, there's also a category index (*Organized Activities for Kids, Swimming Pool, Pets Okay*, etc.) to speed the research process. (Northwest Parent Publishing)

BRITISH COLUMBIA: Strathcona Park Lodge, Campbell River, Vancouver Island

Reservations/Information: 604-286-3122

PROFILE: The Lodge is located in the center of Vancouver Island, perched upon the crystal clear waters of Upper Campbell Lake and framed by snow-capped mountains, This 160-acre Outdoor Education Centre has been in operation since 1960.

In "rustic but modern" waterfront cabins or three-story chalets with individual balconies, up to 150 guests share this private wilderness with grouse, wolves, deer and black bear. The list of activities is long, from Backpacking to Zip Line (a ropes course) and includes canoeing, kayaking, map and compass skills, minimum-impact camping, nature walks, orienteering, an indoor rockwall, winter camping and much more. The lodge is open year-round. Meals, which cost extra, are served buffet-style at common tables, creating a friendly, casual atmosphere.

PROGRAMS: A six-day *Family Adventure* program, geared to families with children between the ages of 6 and 13, is offered on selected summer weeks, though families are welcome to come at any time. During the family weeks expect to take a ropes course, go canoeing and kayaking, join a full-day canoe excursion with an optional overnight and learn about orienteering and rock climbing. An intergenerational Elderhostel (see page 31) program also operates during the summer months. All of the programs are designed so that grown-ups and kids can share the joys of nature and adventure together. There are also on-going summer camps for children ages 10 and older, which need to be reserved in advance. Strathcona Park Lodge is ideal for family reunions.

PRICES: For a family of four, lodge rooms range from $70-$100/night, cabins from $105 to $140/night. There is a discount of 20 percent from mid-September through November. The seventh night is always free. Meals average $30/day/adult, half-price for children 3 to 12.

CARIBBEAN/CENTRAL AMERICA

BELIZE: Maya Mountain Lodge & Educational Field Station, San Ignacio
Reservations/Information: 011-501-92-2164 Fax: 011-501-92-2029

PROFILE: In the English-speaking, Central American country of Belize, a land of rain forests, exotic birds and Mayan ruins, Maya Mountain Lodge offers an extraordinarily appealing experience. Located in the foothills of Mountain Pine Ridge, horseback riding, mountain biking, canoeing and hiking are all possible. A variety of accommodations ranging from comfortable cottages to bunkrooms are offered. Cottages are situated in a tropical setting, decorated with regional crafts and have private bathrooms with hot and cold water (safe for drinking) and fans. Each of the eight cottages has a double bed and a set of bunk beds.

PROGRAMS: Hosts Bart and Suzi Mickler, themselves parents of five, describe what's on the agenda: "From treasure hunts and listening to stories about the rain forest to contributing to a paper called the *Rainforest Daily* ... participating in a puppet show dealing with "issues of the rain forest," collaborating with Belizean families in a conservation project, learning about tropical birds and plants, jungle survival, cooking local dishes, working with clay after visiting a Mayan pottery, etc.." Adventures include "swimming in mountain pools, visiting ancient Mayan cities or motoring up jungle rivers in a dugout canoe."

PRICES: All-inclusive, per person, land prices begin at $339/two-nights/three-days and $598/four-nights/five-days. In summer and during special promotional periods, one child per adult sharing a room is absolutely free. Grandparents are encouraged to bring their grandchildren. Rates include airport transfers. (As we go to press, new taxes in Belize may significantly affect these rates.)

BOOKED FOR TRAVEL

Jaguar in the Rain Forest, a *Just for a Day Book*, reaches out and grabs the young reader from page one. "Imagine you are climbing a ragged tree trunk hand over hand. You are speckled in sunlight that warms you and changes you till . . . You are climbing higher and higher, paw over paw, gripping with curved claws. You are larger and stronger than ever, covered in fur — golden fur, speckled with a dark pattern all your own." In your new feline persona, you prowl through the jungle, hunting. Together, author Joanne Ryder and illustrator Michael Rothman create a believable picture of life in the rain forest through the eyes of a jaguar. (Morrow)

BRITISH VIRGIN ISLANDS: Biras Creek, Virgin Gorda
Reservations/Information: 800-608-9661/809-494-3555

PROFILE: Secluded, serene and low-key, Biras Creek is bordered by the Atlantic Ocean, Caribbean Sea and Sir Francis Drake Channel. Its 32 suites, which can accommodate up to four people, have living rooms and large outdoor balconies. You and your children will love the spacious outdoor garden shower that accompanies each unit. Set on 140 acres with dramatic coastlines, Biras Creek offers miles of scenic, marked nature trails. This is a place to go when you want to chill out, not a place to go to if you crave action. There's a minimum age of 6 for children.

PROGRAMS: As Biras Creek is accessible only by boat, it's no wonder that the emphasis here is on water. The resort provides complimentary snorkeling trips and a variety of small craft. The staff will gladly take you out and teach you how to man your ship if you're not quite ready to assume the role of captain. On land, you can bicycle (bikes, including children's sized bikes, come with each suite), hike along nature trails or go for a nature tour with the resort gardener and admire the inhabitants of the bird sanctuary. Though there's no formal kids' program, the resort's guest assistants (GAs) happily step in to give parents a break, organizing treasure hunts, hermit crab races and other amusements for the young guests.

PRICES: The *Summer Family Vacation* package, from mid-April to mid-December, offers great value. In addition to three meals a day (with an early dinner option and special menu for kids), families with up to two children will be housed in two adjoining suites for the price of one: $3,665/seven-night stay. Winter rates begin at $395/night/suite. All rates include all meals and additional features (which vary according to the package you select).

BOOKED FOR TRAVEL

According to Carroll B. Fleming, author of **Adventuring in the Caribbean:** *The Sierra Club Travel Guide to Forty Islands of the Caribbean Sea*, "Choosing a destination. . . may be the most difficult part of preparation." Fleming goes on to recount that Columbus himself said of his own Caribbean travels, "I saw so many islands that I hardly knew to which I should go first." This solid travel manual should go a long way toward helping the would-be Caribbean visitor not only choose the right island, but also find the most rewarding sights and activities while there. Not limited to the fit and athletic, this is a good book for the curious tourist with eclectic tastes who wants a broader range of holiday experiences than a sojourn at a resort provides. (Sierra Club)

BRITISH VIRGIN ISLANDS: Bitter End Yacht Club, Virgin Gorda

Reservations/Information: 800-872-2392/809-494-2746

PROFILE: Known far and wide as a world-class sailing resort, Bitter End Yacht Club also offers opportunities galore for families who fancy the idea of an eco-vacation. Guests can stay in the hillside chalets, hillside or beachside villas, or on a moored Freedom-30 sailboat that sleeps up to six. Not all of the accommodations have air-conditioning.

Sailing is the focus, and kids ages 7 to 17 are encouraged to join the *Junior Sailing* program . There are also a swimming pool, boat trips, great scuba diving and snorkeling. Movies are shown several times a day on a large video screen next to the dining room. Guests report that the reef tour in a submergible plexiglass aquascope should be a required family activity. Though Bitter End is not recommended for families with children under the age of 7, teenagers rave about their visits here.

PROGRAMS: The resort calls its outdoor study vacation programs *Envirotropical Adventures.* Among the choices are excursions to the bird sanctuary at Anegada Island, to the tidal pools and giant granite boulders at The Baths, snorkeling at Statia Reef and exploring the rain forest at Tortola's Sage Mountain National Park. On all occasions, members of the resort staff are ready and willing to act as guides and mentors. Families are encouraged to participate in these programs together. During the summer months and over some holiday periods, a *Junior Sailing* program is operated for children.

PRICES: A number of all-inclusive package plans offer free lodging and activities for kids during the summer. In high season, an average daily rate for a family of four is $745, the 8-day/7-night *Admiral's Package* is $5,215. In low season prices drop to $570 and $3,990 respectively.

HONDURAS: Anthony's Key Resort, Roatan, Bay Island
Reservations/Information: 800-443-0717/305-666-1997

PROFILE: Encircled by the longest barrier reef in the Americas, Anthony's Key Resort, off the Honduran coast in the Caribbean Sea, calls itself the "original eco-tourism destination." There are two worlds here: a tropical jungle fringed with palm trees and a shimmering underwater kingdom populated by multitudes of iridescent fish.

This is your quintessential dive resort. It has 50 rooms in cozy bungalows, with dive boats heading out several times day and night.

On the water's surface, guests can windsurf, canoe, or use a paddleboat. Horseback riding is also popular.

PROGRAMS: For many, the dolphin programs operated in conjunction with the Institute for Marine Sciences are the resort's main draw. There's a six-day *Dolphin Discovery Camp* for kids ages 8 to 14, with many hands-on dolphin encounters (some of which parents may join). There are also snorkeling lessons and hikes through Carambola Botanical Garden. An incredible experience for any child! Cost for the *Dolphin Discovery Camp* is approximately $500/child with sibling discounts; it's assumed that children are lodging with parents. Swimming, snorkeling or diving next to dolphins are options for adults.

PRICES: All-inclusive dive packages begin at about $910/adult/week. Daily rates range from $135 to $185/night. Children under 12 sharing with parents are charged $40/day, ages 12 to 15, $50/day. Families with younger children might consider taking a Rascals in Paradise *Family Week* (see page 74) here, when activities and babysitting are included for all ages.

BOOKED FOR TRAVEL

Don C. Reed worked for 15 years as a diver in Marine World/Africa USA in California. During that time he became intimately acquainted with the ways of dolphins. **The Dolphins and Me** is a fascinating chronicle of his experiences which is sure to capture young imaginations and shed light on the world of one of the best-loved creatures on our planet. (Sierra Club)

U.S. VIRGIN ISLANDS: The Buccaneer, St. Croix
Reservations/Information: 800-255-3881/809-773-2100/809-778-8215

PROFILE: A converted 300-acre sugar plantation, The Buccaneer boasts three beaches, an 18-hole championship golf course, eight tennis courts, full-service spa, state-of-the-art fitness center and four restaurants. All accommodations feature small refrigerators, whether you select a standard room or a cottage suite.

PROGRAMS: For eco-travelers, The Buccaneer offers botanical walks through the tropical rain forest, sailing and snorkeling at Buck Island Reef (the U.S.'s only underwater National Park), a naturalist-led hike along Salt River, exploration of the unique ecosystem of the resort's Grotto Beach, and, from mid-July to late September, the chance to volunteer for a sea turtle research project. As you might expect, water sports are particularly popular.

Pirate's Playhouse, a children's program for kids ages 5 to 12, runs daily from 10 a.m. to 2 p.m, from April through mid-September. It includes nature walks, exploring the eco-system at Grotto Beach, trips to the beach and other adventures. Special half-price dinners and a kids menu are available. Babysitters are on-hand for $6/hour.

PRICES: Daily rates, which include a full breakfast, range from about $200 to $375 for standard rooms. Suites are $325 to $425 in high season and about 20 percent lower in the off-season. There are attractively-priced weeklong *Family Packages* which feature accommodations in a two-room suite, and *Eco-packages* which include all of the above activities.

BOOKED FOR TRAVEL

"Beyond the ken of mortal men, beneath the wind and waves, There lies a land of shells and sand, of chasms, crags and caves, Where coral castles climb and soar, where swaying seaweeds grow, And all around without a sound the ocean currents flow." So begins Graeme Base's **The Sign of the Seahorse: *A Tale of Greed and High Adventure in Two Acts**.* If you're acquainted with other Base works (e.g., *Animalia, The Eleventh Hour*), you won't be disappointed in this latest offering. There's romance, villainy and a quest — with an underlying lesson in marine biology and ecology — set to a sprightly poetic meter. Best of all are the highly imaginative, humorous and lavish illustrations. Kids will like perusing the map on the endpapers, which shows the ocean floor and the routes followed by the various characters in the story. An A+ for all ages. (Abrams)

U.S VIRGIN ISLANDS: Chenay Bay Beach Resort, St. Croix
Reservations/Information: 800-548-4457/809-773-2918

PROFILE: You'll forget all of the cares of civilization from the moment you enter your lovely, fully-equipped, air conditioned West Indian-style one-bedroom cottage (there are 51 in all) under the palms amid 30-acres of secluded grounds. All is calm along Chenay Bay's half-mile white sand beach and you could easily spend your whole vacation relaxing in the sun. On the other hand, you could easily spend your vacation snorkeling, kayaking, hiking, windsurfing (there's a windsurfing school on the premises which is well-frequented by visiting teens) or playing tennis.

PROGRAMS: Cruzan Kidz is designed for children ages 3 to 12 and runs weekdays from 9 a.m. to 1 p.m. during Christmas, President's Week, Easter and throughout June, July and August. Among the host of activities are tennis, kayaking, snorkeling, swimming, hiking and shell collecting. When the program is not in operation, two hours of complimentary babysitting (normally $6/hour) are offered daily.

You will want to take your kids over to the Buck Island Reef National Monument. If your children are over the age of 6, the St. Croix Environmental Association (809-773-1989) can take you on a guided hike over at Salt River where you'll find the island's largest mangrove forests and a number of endangered species of plants and animals.

PRICES: From mid-April through mid-December, a second room for children in the cottages is half-price. Book five nights and the sixth is free. Children under 18 not only stay free when they share with adults, they also eat free. High season nightly rates range from $175 to $225, low season from $140 to $190. Family units of two connecting cottages cost $1,260 to $1,578/seven nights in the summer, from $1,942 to $2,467 in winter.

CHAPTER 7

DAY TRIPS & ANIMAL ENCOUNTERS

From the moment we began researching this book, the incredible choices we found whetted our appetites. Like many of you, we don't always have the time and/or dollars to visit all of the wondrous and exotic places we've described. So we looked in our own backyard to see how close we could get to nature. Much to our surprise, our city (known best for its concrete not its nature-oriented experiences) offered us a bounty of opportunity—from the greenery at the Brooklyn Botanic Garden to the wild forests of Riverdale's Wave Hill, from the New York Wildlife Conservation Park (Bronx Zoo) to Brooklyn's Aquarium and Manhattan's own Central Park — there's no lack of green moments away from the sidewalks of New York.

You may find that just a small taste of nature will lure your family into one of the longer trips found in this book. Whether you pass by in the car en route to somewhere else, make the stop your day's ultimate destination or happen to be staying near the places we list, we're certain that you and your kids will remember these outings long into the future. To simplify matters, we've listed out choices by state, in alphabetical order.

When passing through **ALABAMA,** stop in *DeSoto Caverns Park* (205-378-7252). This 80-acre park, located near Sylacauga, is most noted for its marble and has mammoth onyx caverns (the Great Onyx Cathedral is larger than a football field). First reports on the cave date back to 1540 and it's said that during the Civil War it was a major gunpowder mining center. There's also a maze, a water-powered rock cutting saw and a chance to pan for gold.

In Huntsville, home of the U.S. Space and Rocket Center, the *Madison County Nature Center* (205-883-9501) features a braille trail among its wooded hiking trails. There's also a covered bridge, a lake and waterfall.

Way up above the 48 states lies **ALASKA**, a state with more than its share of natural wonders. Visitors to the *Alaska Chilkat Bald Eagle Preserve* (907-766-2491, 20 miles from Haines) are never disappointed. From fall into winter, the site is a mecca for birdwatchers who come to watch the largest gathering of American bald eagles in the world. In spring and summer it's nesting season for the eagles while myriad other forms of wildlife also appear, including whales, terns, moose and bear.

Take a unique voyage with *Verde Canyon Railroad* (800-293-7245/520-639-0010) of Clarkdale, **ARIZONA**. Pass by some of the area's most breathtaking high desert scenery in Sedona and the Verde Valley, from red sandstone pillars to fields of wildflowers, all seen from the train's open-air viewing cars. In winter months an Eagle Watch runs from November through March, and a narration on the scenery and natural history is featured during the 40-mile roundtrip between Clarkdale and Perkinsville year-round.

A mere 35 miles north of Tucson is *Biosphere 2* (520-602-6200), the facility that studies our planet's ecosystems. Though tours don't enter the experimental areas, they are particularly informative and interesting.

BOOKED FOR TRAVEL

Places to Go with Children is a series of books that are packed with a mix of indoor and outdoor escapades — museums, playgrounds, theme parks, nature outings, sporting possibilities — kids and parents can enjoy visiting at every season. Destinations in the series include: *the Southwest. New England, the Delaware Valley, Washington, D.C., Colorado, Miami and South Florida, Orlando and Central Florida, Puget Sound, Northern California* and *Southern California.* Each listing contains the pertinent details needed for planning a visit together with information on age-appropriateness. No information on lodging is provided. (Chronicle)

Families rave about the fun they have at *Crater of Diamonds State Park* (501-285-3113) in Murfreesboro in southeast **ARKANSAS**. This one-time gem-bearing volcanic area is the only U.S. diamond area open to the public where visitors can dig for diamonds. Believe it or not, even young children have met with success here!

If you're looking to visit a national park but can't get out west, check out *Hot Springs National Park*, just 50 miles southwest of Little Rock, the only national park located in the middle of a city.

On **CALIFORNIA**'s Monterey Peninsula in Carmel, *Otter-Mobile* (408-625-9782) welcomes kids on its host of daily trips in the area and will be pleased to customize one for your family. There are nature walking tours plus trips that observe eagles or elephant seals.

Check out *Starlight*, Santa Catalina Island's Discovery Tours' (800-995-4386) semi-submersible vessel, the first of its kind in southern California. During both day and night departures, up to 36 passengers can view the island's magnificent undersea gardens, previously only accessible to divers.

As you pass through **COLORADO**, stop at *Winter Park Resort* (970-726-5514). In winter take a two-hour snowshoe tour along the forested trails at the mountain; in spring, summer or fall, join a gentle backcountry tour to learn about local history, native plants and animals.

Anyone in the vicinity of Pueblo will want to visit *The Greenway and Nature Center of Pueblo* (719-545-9114). Its highly regarded Raptor Center, managed by the University of Southern Colorado, provides convalescent care for injured birds of prey. The naturalist programs emphasize the vital importance of raptors and other wildlife in our world and focus on the area's natural and cultural history and conservation efforts. Located in Rock Canyon on the banks of the Arkansas River one mile from town, the area is a delicate blend of aquatic, piparian, transition and semi-arid grassland habitats. There is a 21-mile River Trails System, several displays and exhibits, bike rentals and eco-camp programs for kids.

If you're in Aspen during the summer, give the *Anderson Ranch Arts Center* a call at 800-525-2722 and see if any of their kids' workshops are scheduled. We especially like those that take kids into the woods to forage for material from which they create works of art.

The *Aspen Center for Environmental Studies*, ACES (970-925-5756), offers a variety of programs year-round for both children and adults several times a week, year-round. Animal Tracking, Bugs, Bugs, Bugs, Wetlands and Wildlife, Antlers and Horns, the World of Bears, Creatures of the Night and Basket Weaving are among the choices for children, ages 8 to 12. The Little Naturalist Program for ages 4 to 5 and 6 to 7 may feature Plant Creations, Fluttery Flyers, Terrific Turtles, Honkers and Quackers, Sneaky Snakes or Makin' Tracks. Adult fare is always offered. In winter, naturalist guided snowshoe walks, a Birds of Prey program and interesting hour-long evening sessions welcome the entire family.

As the home state of the *National Audubon Society* headquarters (203-869-5272, see page 36), in **CONNECTICUT** you'll find many places "for the birds" around the state, beginning with the center itself on Riversville Road in Greenwich , where eight miles of trails, (including a Discovery Trail), and a backyard wildlife habitat await.

Not far from Hartford, in Rocky Hill, check out *Dinosaur State Park* (203-529-8423) where hundreds of ancient dinosaur tracks remain intact and visitors are invited to make casts. The only catch is that you must bring your own veggie oil and plaster of paris.

Located one hour from either the east or west coasts of southern **FLORIDA** in Clewiston is *Kissimmee Billie Swamp Safari*, a "world untouched by modern civilization." Operated at the Big Cypress Seminole Indian Reservation of Florida (800-949-6101), visit the Reptile Center, take an airboat ride, paddle a canoe, hop on a swam buggy or walk the Swamp Trail, where you're apt to spot buffalo, antelope, panthers or hawks. Overnight stays and night safaris are also possible.

Just 10 minutes from Marco Island is *Briggs Nature Center* (813-775-8569), where visitors can take out canoes, join a pontoon boat tour or a sunset bird watch or simply survey the looking-glass walkway that winds beneath virginal cypress and southwest pines (located within the 11,000 acre Rookery Bay National Estuarine Research Reserve).

Believe it or not, Walt Disney World offers an incredible array of nature study possibilities. At Discovery Island, an 11-acre sanctuary where animals roam free, you can watch exotic birds, explore a rain forest, trek through tropical foliage and see Muntjac deer, Galapagos tortoises and Patagonian Cavy. A number of programs are run for youngsters (407-824-3784). Meanwhile, over at the new Disney Institute (800-496-6337), several environmentally-aware courses are featured, from Bird Watcher's Paradise to Swamp Party. There are special programs for young guests ages 10 to 17. Children ages 7 to 9 can participate in the Disney Day Camp Program which also features its fair share of outdoor fun. We're hopeful that as the Institute grows, family programs will be introduced.

You can stay overnight or visit for the day at *Callaway Gardens* (800-CALLAWAY/706-663-5153 - for program information) in Pine Mountain, **GEORGIA**, to partake in any of its year-round events from nocturnal nature walks to family nature hunts. While on the property, don't miss the famed Horticultural Center or the Cecil B. Day Butterfly Garden.

If you're near the Olympic city of Atlanta, check out the *Chattahoochee Nature Center* (404-992-2055) in Roswell with its hiking trails and interpretive center. Kids love the treehouse and the wildlife rehabilitation programs, where small wild animals are always on hand to see and touch.

Leave the highrise hotels of Waikiki behind when you visit *Sea Life Park* (800-767-8046) in **HAWAII**, 15 miles from Honolulu. While taking in breathtaking backdrops of Makapu'u Point and the Koolau Mountains, visitors can enter a Hawaiian reef tank, walk through a Sea Bird Sanctuary, observe at a Sea Lion Feeding Pool and check out a Turtle Lagoon.

Back in town, ask about *Royal Hawaiian Cruises* (800-852-4183) whale-watching cruises on the *Navtek I* that begin operation each January and feature expert narration by professional naturalists. At the company's Whale Watch Information Center in Honolulu, visitors learn about humpback whales and their curious behaviors.

When you're not on a river in **IDAHO**, consider a visit underground. Take an hour-long *Sierra Silver Mine Tour* (208-752-5151) at a real working mine. (Sorry, no kids under 4). Next door is the *Wallace District Mining Museum* (208-753-7151) in the town of Wallace, not far from Coeur d'Alene.

Yes, you can play in Peoria, **ILLINOIS**. The *Peoria Wildlife Prairie* (309-676-0998), 10 miles west of town, is home to a variety of animals indigenous to the state, including bison, whitetailed deer and live wolves. There's a playground and petting area for more domesticated critters.

In the town of Elizabeth in southern **INDIANA**, see the north American buffalo herd at Needmore Buffalo Farm (812-968-3473); ask about the hayrides that take you through the fields.

In the western part of the state in Battle Ground, howl with the wolves any Friday night at *Wolf Park* (317-567-2265). See the wolves at close range and also observe a small herd of bison.

You can still see the Bridges of Madison County, six of which remain intact in the state of **IOWA**. Call the Chamber of Commerce of Winterset at 515-765-4586 for the exact locations.

At *Maquoketa Caves State Park* (319-652-5833), find large limestone caves, hiking trails, a natural bridge and a 17-ton rock perilously balanced on a cliff. The town of Maquoketa was formerly a stopping point for wagon trains who loaded up with supplies before crossing the river and heading west.

Though Richmond, **KENTUCKY**, is best known as a scene of a major Civil War battle, it is also the home of the *Hummel Planetarium and Space Theater* (606-622-1547). Located on the Eastern Kentucky University campus, this is one of the most sophisticated facilities in the United States.

Any visit to New Orleans, **LOUISIANA**, should include time at the *Louisiana Science and Nature Center* (504-246-5672) where there's a wildlife preserve, an IMAX theater and hands-on backyard nature trails through wetlands and forests.

Due west of New Orleans, in Lafayette, the *Lafayette Natural History Museum & Planetarium* (318-241-8448) offers a roster of field trips that include Sky Events, Bird Walks and Night Hikes on the last Saturday evening of each month. Families with children ages 6 and older are invited to tramp through the darkness in search of owls, raccoons, armadillos, frogs and other creatures of the night.

MooseMainea breaks out each spring at, where else, *Moosehead Lake* (207-695-2702) in **MAINE**. Tourists traveling by van, boat or even floatplane, can join a guided moose safari. Last year there were a record 5,288 moose sightings.

Need more ideas on what to do in Maine? Call *Experience Maine* (800-21-MAINE/617-899-0881), a customized itinerary-planning service run by Marjorie Bride and Betty Scott, who have raised five children between them. Whether you're looking for culture, time in the outdoors, the perfect place to stay or the most succulent lobster, their aim is "to plan the perfect itinerary, day to day, minute to minute."

On the **MASSACHUSETTS** island of Martha's Vineyard, the *Kayak Company* (508-627-0151) in Tisbury invites kids of all ages to discover the area's wildlife on one of the "most peaceful paddles around the most scenic part of the island".

Calling itself "Cape Cods' Floating Classroom, an on-the-water environmental education experience for all ages," *Hyannis Whale Watcher Cruises* (800-287-0374/508-362-6088) in Barnstable offers daily departures on its high speed M/V *Whale Watcher*. You're guaranteed to sight whales or you'll be able to sail again, free.

Take a bike or hike in **MICHIGAN**'s Huron Swamp in Indian Springs at the *Metropark Nature Center* (313-625-7280). See the wetlands first-hand along the bike paths or nature trails and don't miss the pond critters table, a sure-fire-kid-pleaser.

In Charlevoix, at *Fisherman's Island State Park* (616-547-6641), it's time to hunt for Petoskey stones, fossil remains of animals that lived in the warm seas at the time of the dinosaurs. These state stones are best seen when they are wet.

Contrast your day at The Mall of America in Bloomington, **MIN-NESOTA,** with a visit to the *Minnesota Valley Wildlife Refuge* (612-854-5900) where your kids will be thrilled with the hands-on computer games and exhibits. In addition to learning how to become a wildlife manger or be the boss on a fire burn, a number of naturalist-led programs are offered.

At *The Raptor Center* (612-624-4745) in St. Paul see live bird demonstrations and view some of the injured birds of prey treated there. Nearby, the *Como Zoo* (612-487-1485) is a small gem with a conservatory and gardens.

Not far from Ludlow's Island Resort (see page 159) is the *International Wolf Center* (800-359-9653) in Ely, adjacent to state's boundary waters area and home to the largest wolf population in the lower 48 states. In close proximity is the heart of Minnesota's Iron Range and *Soudan Underground Mine State Park* (218-753-2245) where the only mine of its type in the world is open to the general public.

On the campus of **MONTANA** State University in Bozeman is the *Museum of the Rockies* (406-DIG DINO), which includes a fascinating dinosaur exhibit where you can learn how to excavate dinosaur bones. There's also a planetarium and summer paleontology field program for children ages 10 and older.

Winter and summer, the *Glacier Institute* (406-888-5215) in Kalispell runs programs for families. The majority of these explorations are appropriate for children about 10 and older.

Dirty, tired and exhilarated is how parents describe their kids after a visit to the *Lost River Reservation* (603-745-8031) in North Woodstock, **NEW HAMPSHIRE.** A three-quarter-mile trip along the river winds in and out of the boulders of a steep-walled gorge. Stick to the self-guided boardwalk path with younger kids, but let the older ones explore and navigate the crevasses on their own.

A visit to the *Science Center of New Hampshire* (603-968-7194) in Holderness is a bit less intrepid. Here you'll find a 200-acre sanctuary for an assortment of injured or orphaned animals who can no longer survive in the wild; indoor and outdoor interactive displays; an underwater viewing window; a turtle island and a special children's activity center. An Up Close Animals session is held daily in summer as are nature cruises on Squam Lake.

Only 26 miles southwest of Grants, **NEW MEXICO,** is *Perpetual Ice Cave* (505-783-4303), a glacier that formed underneath a lava flow.

A true gem, the *Geology Museum and Meteorite Museum* (505-277-4204) of the University of New Mexico in Albuquerque is a rich depository of minerals, dinosaurs, fossils and fluorescence. While on campus, see if you can visit the biology department's Greenhouse or the Observatory in the Physics and Astronomy Building.

The *Living Desert Zoological and Botanical State Park* (505-887-5516) in Carlsbad is a sprawling botanical zoo with mountain lions, quail, badgers, javelinas and roadrunners. Guests are permitted to feed the mule deer.

Walk or take a boat ride through **NEW YORK**'s *Ausable Chasm* (518-834-7454) in the Champlain Valley, a gorge cut by the Ausable River at the end of the last Ice Age. Nearby, the *Essex County Fish Hatchery* (518-597-3844) in Crown Point welcomes visitors year-round.

In the lower Hudson Valley, the *Westmoreland Sanctuary* (914-666-8448) in Mount Kisco, the *Manitoga Nature Preserve* (914-424-3812) in Garrison-on-Hudson, the *Catskill Fly Fishing Center & Museum* (914-439-4810) in Livingston Manor, *Ice Cave Mountain* (914-47-7989) in Ellenville and *Five Rivers Environmental Center* (518-457-6092) in Delmar are all worth a visit.

In the Pisgah National Forest in **NORTH CAROLINA**, the *Cradle of Forestry* (704-877-3130) is the birthplace of modern forestry in America. A special children's area teaches about conservation with a number of exciting exhibits and demonstrations. Loggers can be found along the forest trails to answer any questions you may have.

At the *Klamath Basin* in Klamath Falls, **OREGON**, pick up a copy of *A Child's Guide to Link River*, a guide to the Nature Society's trails in the Link River Bird Sanctuary and Small Animal Refuge. The entire county is filled with natural wonders, including Lava Beds National

Monument, the legendary Crater Lake and more. For details, contact the county Department of Tourism at 800-445-6728 or 503-884-0666.

BOOKED FOR TRAVEL

Globe Pequot Press has introduced a series of **Family Adventure Guides:** *Great Things to See and Do for the Entire Family.* As we go to press we've had the chance to look at the following titles: Northern Califorant, Southern California, Connecticut, Indiana, Oregon, Tennessee, Virginia and Wisconsin. More states are being added each season. These are not guides to adventure vacations. Rather, they cover congenial family activities. We've perused the guides and in each case found ourselves caught up in the author's infectious excitement for the given state's family-friendly offerings, hardly surprising since all are local experts as well as being parents. The guides work well both for locals and out-of-staters, especially when driving. The extensive indices are a real boon.

In **PENNSYLVANIA,** sight bald eagles along the *Upper Delaware Scenic and Recreational River* during the day and listen to speakers from the New York Audubon Society in the evenings. One day programs begin at 10 a.m. during the winter season when the frozen lakes and rivers force the eagles to migrate southward. Ask for a copy of "Bald Eagles in the Delaware River Valley: A Guide For Safe And Successful Eagle Watching." Packages, which include lodging, such as the one at the Best Western Inn at Hunts Landing in Matamoras (717-296-6025), are also offered.

Along the Ashley River near Charleston, **SOUTH CAROLINA,** is the low-country plantation *Middleton Place* (803-766-8430). Recently the woodland area has been open to the public through its Water Wood and Wildlife program, a series of two-hour day or evening nature walks led by the resident wildlife biologist. Half- and full-day expeditions of Bulls Island, Santee River Delta, Bluff Plantation or Edisto Island are among the pickings of the tours offered by Charleston *Wildlife Watch* (803-762-1947), which promises "fun and discovery for all ages" according to naturalist/guide Virginia Christian Beach.

The endangered Kemp ridley sea turtle is a must-see on South Padre Island, **TEXAS**. *Sea Turtle, Inc.* (512-943-2544), founded by Ila Loetscher, The Turtle Lady, sponsors shows and visits year-round at what is now their permanent home.

Fossil Rim Wildlife Center (800-245-0771/817-897-2960) in Glen Rose is a terrific alternative for anyone who doesn't anticipate having the opportunity to visit Africa. The facility, 3,000 acres of rolling hills and African-like savannahs, is home to both native animals and wildlife from around the world. During a scenic drive tour you view exotic, threatened and endangered animals. This well-managed conservation effort, staffed with exceptional rangers, allows visitors to get to get close to zebra and giraffes. There are guided, behind-the-scenes, mountain bike and conservation tours to select from. One thirteen-year-old said of the tour, "A visit here is an essential thing for most teenagers. I could go on forever about its beauty and wonderfulness."

BOOKED FOR TRAVEL

Anyone contemplating a trip to **UTAH** should head for the nearest bookstore and pick up a copy of the *Compass American Guide: Utah* by Tom and Gayen Wharton. With 15 maps and outstanding photographs, the book reads more like a novel than a travel guide and will lead your family through a number of outdoor adventures you might otherwise miss out on. (Fodors)

At *Bolton Valley Resort* (802-434-2131) in **VERMONT**, Mountain Ecology Tours take place at the Nature Center. Daily programs are run during the winter and summer seasons and may focus on edible plants, nature photography and the like. Guided nature walks (on snowshoes in winter), are offered for the entire family.

Wildlife viewing is always spectacular in **WASHINGTON** state. To learn where and how, call 800-890-5493 for a free copy of the state's seasonally published Activity Guide.

Limekiln State Park on San Juan Island, with its view of Victoria, B.C., was the nation's first whale-watching park. With three resident pods of whales, the best viewing time is from June to August. For more information, contact the San Juan Island Visitor & Convention bureau at 360-468-3663.

Dungeness Spit (360-457-8451), near Port Townsend in the Strait of Juan de Fuca, is a haven for shore birds and myriad waterfowl during spring and fall migration periods. Year-round, harbor seals can be seen along the five-mile beach trail

Mount St. Helens is the place to learn first-hand about the devastation nature can cause. Hear about recovery and reforestation at the *Forest Learning Center* (360-414-3439) in Longview, where a volcano-themed playground has been built next to the avalanche debris.

Assateague Island National Seashore spans the states of **MARYLAND** and **VIRGINIA**. The barrier island is a marshland area where herds of wild ponies wander. Each July, during the Wild Pony Round-up, the ponies swim across the shallow bay into Chincoteague.

Watch bears wrestle, roll, forage, fight and play at **WYOMING's** *Grizzly Discovery Center* (800-257-2570/406-646-7001) in West Yellowstone. Some of the bears here were born in captivity, others were discovered undernourished or injured or have been labeled as "problems." All are studied here in an effort to guarantee the grizzly's survival. Vsitors are offered "a unique opportunity to observe, learn about and appreciate this magnificent animal." Children can crawl into a replicated bear den, touch grizzly bear fur, compare themselves to a grizzly bear and learn first-hand the consequences of human/bear conflict.

There's no lack of exciting fare in the **CARIBBEAN**. *Stingray City*, off the coast of **Grand Cayman**, has become quite famous as the place where man meets ray. Red Sail Sports (800-255-6425-US/809-949-8745) sails there from the Hyatt Regency dock, with a boatload of snorkelers and a picnic lunch. About 20 or so rays congregate in the shallow waters of the barrier reef, waiting to be fed, and willingly fraternize with snorkelers and divers.

Children love meeting the tiny hatchlings and 500 pound behemoths at the *Cayman Turtle Farm* (809-949-3894), the world's only green sea turtle nursery. It's easy to get to for anyone staying in the vicinity of Seven Mile Beach. In addition to affording a delightful outing for tourists, the farm is very much a breeding and research facility. Other inhabitants of the farm include agoutis, iguanas, Cayman green parrots and American crocodiles.

The *Barbados Wildlife Reserve* (809-422-8826) is an easy drive from the beach resorts of the West Shore and was the highlight of our island tour during a recent visit to **Barbados**. Troupes of green monkeys, lumbering tortoises (the practical monkeys use them as benches while they eat), dainty brocket deer (with their fawns peacefully nibbling in the mahogany groves), spectacled caimans (snoozing in the streams) — we saw them all. Other animals on the reserve are otters, mongoose, wallabies and more.

Martinique's *Vallee des Papillons* (011-596-78-19-19) is a butterfly habitat set in the midst of lush, tropical gardens which flourish alongside the romantic ruins of l'Habitation Anse Latouche, destroyed during the 1902 eruption of Mont Pelee. Numerous species of vividly-hued butterflies flit freely about the greenhouse. Little kids should be especially entranced, especially when they learn that the average life of a butterfly is only four or five days.

In 1988, *Atlantis Submarines* began showing ordinary people the world beneath the sea that once only certified scuba divers had access to. Today, Atlantis offers "dive" sites in **Aruba, Nassau, Barbardos, Grand Cayman, St. Thomas/St. John, Cancun, Guam** and on three islands in **Hawaii**, including Kona on the Big Island where it first began. Atlantis recently received the Gold Award for excellence in environmental education from the Pacific Asia Travel Association for its "Living Classroom" program. We and our kids have explored the Barcader Reef in Aruba, Buck Island National Wildlife Preserve in the U.S. Virgin Islands, and the natural and man-made reefs in Cancun. As certified divers, we're always pleased and surprised at how much we learn each and every time. Tours differ at each location. To learn more, call 800-253-0493 for Caribbean destinations (800-887-8571 for Grand Cayman) or 800-548-6262 in Hawaii. Children must be four years old.

Appendices

BEST BETS

ALL AGES & FAMILY CONFIGURATIONS
In this section, absolutely any age child and all adults will feel welcome and accommodated.

Educational Organizations
National Wildlife Federation

Tour Operators & Specialized Travel Services
Abercrombie & Kent
AWE
Family Explorations
Off The Beaten Path
Oh, To Be In England
Rascals in Paradise
Tread Lightly

On The Water
Class VI River Runners
Temptress Voyages

Stay & Play
Little St. Simons Island
Pocono Environmental
    Education Center
The Nature Place
Wildflower Inn
Maya Mountain Lodge

BEST WHEN TRAVELING WITH BABIES
We've defined babies as children under 2. Those organizations and places listed below can easily arrange for childcare, private babysitting and necessary equipment such as cribs and highchairs.

Educational Organizations
National Wildlife Federation

Tour Operators & Specialized Travel Services
Abercrombie & Kent
AWE
Family Explorations
Off The Beaten Path

Oh, To Be In England
Rascals in Paradise
Tread Lightly

On The Water
Class VI River Runners
Temptress Voyages

Stay & Play
Little St. Simons Island
Pocono Environmental Education
   Center
The Nature Place
Keystone Resort

The Tyler Place
Grand Targhee
Wildflower Inn
Maya Mountain Lodge
The Buccaneer

FOR THOSE WITH TODDLERS /PRESCHOOLERS

For this grouping, you need to read each listing carefully as the programs and facilities for this age group (between 2 and 5 years) varies greatly. There is much more available for a 4-year-old than there is for a 2-year-old.

Educational Organizations
Appalachian Mountain Club
National Wildlife Federation
Sierra Club
UNEXSO

Tour Operators & Specialized Travel Services
Abercrombie & Kent
AWE
Arctic Treks
Born Free Safaris
Family Explorations
Journeys
Micato Safaris
Natural Habitat Adventures
Off The Beaten Path
Oh, To Be In England
Rascals in Paradise
Tread Lightly

On The Water
Class VI River Runners

Premier Cruise Lines
Temptress Voyages

Stay & Play
Hyatt Resorts
Little St. Simons Island
Telemark Inn
Mohonk Mountain House
Pocono Environmental Education
   Center
The Tyler Place
The Wildflower Inn
Wintergreen
The Nature Place
Keystone Resort Resort
Ludlow's Island Resort
Deer Creek Resort
Oglebay Resort
Grand Targhee
Maya Mountain Lodge
The Buccaneer
Cheany Bay Beach Resort

IF TRAVELING WITH SCHOOL AGE CHILDREN
Every listing in this book is appropriate for parents traveling with school-age children.

Educational Organizations
Appalachian Mountain Club
Canyonlands Field Institute
Chewonki Foundation
Cottonwood Gulch Foundation
Denver Museum of Natural History
Dinamation International Society
Discovery Tours
FAMILYHOSTEL
Friends of the River
NAS Nature Odysseys
National Wildlife Federation
Nature Conservancy
Sierra Club
UNEXSO
Wilderness Southeast

Tour Operators & Specialized Travel Services
Alaska Wildland Adventures
Arctic Treks
Born Free Safaris
Grandtravel
Journeys
Micato Safaris
Natural Habitat Adventures
Nature Expeditions International
OAT
Super Natural Adventures
Tread Lightly

On the Water
Class VI River Runners
Coastal Adventures

ECHO
Galapagos Network
Premier Cruise Lines
ROW
Temptress Voyages

Stay & Play
Hyatt Resorts
Cheeca Lodge
Little St. Simons Island
The Telemark Inn
Mohonk Mountain House
Pocono Environmental Education
  Center
The Tyler Place
Wildflower Inn
Wintergreen Resort
The Nature Place
Keystone Resort Resort
Ludlow's Island Resort
Deer Creek Resort
Oglebay Resort
Grand Targhee
Mauna Lani Bay Hotel
Lake Upsata Guest Ranch
Sundance
Strathcona Park Lodge
Maya Mountain Lodge
Biras Creek
Bitter End Yacht Club
The Buccaneer
Chenay Bay Beach Resort
Anthony's Key Resort

WHEN WITH TEENAGERS

As parents of teenagers, we've carefully chosen those organizations and places where we believe teens and their parents will all return from vacation anxious to travel with each other again. In the Stay & Play category this does not always mean that there will be special teen activities but rather that youngsters in this age group will easily be able to meet each other and socialize without parents worrying about where their teens may be.

Educational Organizations
Canyonlands Field Institute
Chewonki Foundation
Cottonwood Gulch Foundation
Denver Museum of Natural History
Dinamation International Society
Discovery Tours
FAMILYHOSTEL
Friends of the River
NAS Nature Odysseys
National Wildlife Federation
Nature Conservancy
Sierra Club
UNEXSO
Wilderness Southeast

Tour Operators & Specialized Travel Services
Alaska Wildland Adventures
Arctic Treks
Born Free Safaris
Journeys
Micato Safaris
Natural Habitat Adventures
Nature Expeditions International
OAT
Super Natural Adventures

On The Water
Coastal Adventures

ECHO
Galapagos Network
Premier Cruise Lines
ROW
Temptress Voyages

Stay & Play
Hyatt Resorts
Cheeca Lodge
Little St. Simons Island
The Telemark Inn
Pocono Environmental Education Center
The Tyler Place
Wildflower Inn
Wintergreen Resort
The Nature Place
Keystone Resort Resort
Ludlow's Island Resort
Deer Creek Resort
Oglebay Resort
Grand Targhee
Mauna Lani Bay Hotel
Lake Upsata Guest Ranch
Sundance
Strathcona Park Lodge
Maya Mountain Lodge
Bitter End Yacht Club
Chenay Bay Beach Resort
Anthony's Key Resort

INTERGENERATIONAL GROUPS

Vacations seem to work best for grandparents and grandchildren when members of both groups find peers with whom to socialize.

Educational Organizations
Appalachian Mountain Club
Canyonlands Field Institute
Elderhostel
FAMILYHOSTEL
NAS Nature Odysseys
Nature Conservancy
Sierra Club
UNEXSO

Tour Operators & Specialized Travel Services
Abercrombie & Kent
Alaska Wildland Adventures
Grandtravel
Natural Habitat Adventures
Nature Expeditions International
Super Natural Adventures

On The Water
ECHO
Galapagos Network
Premier Cruise Lines
ROW
Temptress Voyages

Stay & Play
Hyatt Resorts
Cheeca Lodge
Little St. Simons Island
The Telemark Inn
Mohonk Mountain House
Pocono Environmental Education
  Center
Wildflower Inn
Wintergreen Resort
The Nature Place
Keystone Resort Resort
Deer Creek Resort
Oglebay Resort
Grand Targhee
Mauna Lani Bay Hotel
Sundance
Strathcona Park Lodge
Maya Mountain Lodge
Biras Creek
Bitter End Yacht Club
The Buccaneer
Chenay Bay Beach Resort
Anthony's Key Resort

MULTIGENERATIONAL FAMILIES

Multigenerational groups often need only themselves to enjoy spectacular vacations. However, we believe that when these types of vacations take place where members of all generations are catered to, you can't go wrong.

Educational Organizations
Canyonland Fields Institute

Denver Museum of Natural History
Discovery Tours

FAMILYHOSTEL
NAS Nature Odysseys
National Wildlife Federation
Sierra Club
UNEXSO
Wilderness Southeast

Tour Operators & Specialized Travel Services
Born Free Safaris
Grandtravel
Journeys
Micato Safaris
Natural Habitat Adventures
Nature Expeditions International
Super Natural Adventures
Tread Lightly

On The Water
Class VI River Runners
Coastal Adventures
ECHO
Galapagos Network
Premier Cruise Lines
ROW
Temptress Voyages

Stay & Play
Hyatt Resorts
Cheeca Lodge
Little St. Simons Island
The Telemark Inn
Mohonk Mountain House
Pocono Environmental Education
    Center
Wildflower Inn
Wintergreen Resort
The Nature Place
Keystone Resort
Ludlow's Island Resort
Deer Creek Resort
Oglebay Resort
Grand Targhee
Mauna Lani Bay Hotel
Lake Upsata Guest Ranch
Sundance
Strathcona Park Lodge
Maya Mountain Lodge
Biras Creek
Bitter End Yacht Club
The Buccaneer
Chenay Bay Beach Resort
Anthony's Key Resort

IF YOU'RE A SINGLE PARENT

We know first-hand that traveling only with our children presents a challenge. We've selected places and tour organizations where single adults should easily be able to make friends, have company at mealtimes and not feel guilty about separate adult and child activities.

Educational Organizations
Appalachian Mountain Club
Canyonlands Field Institute
Chewonki Foundation
Discovery Tours

FAMILYHOSTEL
National Wildlife Federation
Sierra Club
UNEXSO
Wilderness Southeast

Tour Operators & Specialized Travel Services
Arctic Treks
Journeys
Super Natural Adventures

On The Water
Coastal Adventures
ECHO
Galapagos Network
Premier Cruise Lines
ROW
Temptress Voyages

Stay & Play
Little St. Simons Island
The Telemark Inn
Mohonk Mountain House
Pocono Environmental Education
    Center
Wildflower Inn
The Nature Place
Deer Creek Resort
Oglebay Resort
Lake Upsata Guest Ranch
Strathcona Park Lodge
Maya Mountain Lodge
Anthony's Key Resort

INDEX

TELL US ABOUT YOUR OWN GREAT NATURE VACATION

We want to hear about the places you've discovered so that we can include them in our next edition.

Please take a minute to complete the following form and return it to:

TWYCH, Travel With Your Children
40 Fifth Avenue, New York, NY 10011.

Your name: _____

Address: _____

_____

Telephone: _____

Name of Property/Tour Operator: _____

Address: _____

_____

Telephone: _____

Describe your "find." We'll contact them directly for details.

Many, many thanks.

Other books published by World Leisure

- **Getting To Know You – 365 questions and activities**
  to enhance relationships by Jeanne McSweeney & Charles Leocha
  A book of intimate questions that get right to the heart of
  successful relationships.
  $6.95

- **Getting To Know Kids in Your Life**
  by Jeanne McSweeney and Charles Leocha
  Interactive questions and activities to really get to know children for
  parents, aunts, uncles, grandparents and anyone who shares time with
  3- to 7-year-olds.
  $6.95

- **A Woman's ABCs of Life – from those who learned the hard way**
  by Beca Lewis Allen
  Inspired advice collected for her daughter helps women expand their
  lives with practical, fun and entering insights about life.
  $6.95

- **Travel Rights** by Charles Leocha
  The book filled with answers to travelers' difficult questions.
  It saves you money and makes travel more hassle-free.
  $7.95

- **Cheap Dates — Boston** by Alexandra Ryan
  A romantic's guide to affordable Boston.
  $9.95

- **Skiing America** by Charles Leocha
  Annually updated guidebook to North America's best ski resorts.
  $18.95

- **Ski Europe** by Charles Leocha
  Guidebook to Europe's top ski resorts.
  $17.95

- **WomenSki** by Claudia Carbone
  Award-winning breakthrough book about why women
  can't ski like men and shouldn't.
  $14.95

All available by calling 1-800-444-2524
or send payment plus $3.75 shipping and handling
to: World Leisure, 177 Paris St., Boston, MA 02128